This book belongs to

_____

Hey there!

We've created a very special book for you called a mindfulness activity book! It's a place where you can do lots of fun activities and practice mindfulness!

In this book, we have different sections where you can explore your feelings and thoughts. There's a section where you can learn how to make yummy treats like smoothies, muffins and even nuggets! There's also a section for mindfulness activities, where you can learn about colouring, deep breathing, creative visualisation and even mindful walking in nature.

But the best part of the book is the reflection section! This is where you can get to know yourself better by writing about your goals, your mood, and even by answering some fun prompts. It's a great way to see how you're feeling each day and to remember all the good things in your life.

So grab your pens, pencils and crayons and let's get started on this fun and exciting journey of mindfulness and creativity!

Date _____

Daily Mood Tracker

This is a chart where you get to track how you're feeling each day. You can tag a smiley face if you're feeling happy, a sad face if you're feeling sad, or a neutral face if you're feeling indifferent. It's a fun way to see how your mood changes over time!

Excited ☐   Happy ☐   Relaxed ☐   Sad ☐   Nervous ☐   Stressed ☐   Angry ☐

Self-reflection

Take some time to think about how you're feeling and what's been going on in your life. Ask yourself "why did I tag myself with this emotion?", and write down your answer below.

_____
_____
_____
_____
_____
_____
_____
_____
_____
_____
_____
_____
_____
_____
_____
_____

Did you know that writing down your feelings can be really helpful? It's like using a magic tool that helps you figure out how you're feeling and why. When you write down your feelings, you can learn more about yourself and feel happier. It can also help you solve problems and feel less worried or scared.

So, remember: writing down your feelings is like using a superpower! It helps you learn more about yourself and feel better inside.

Colouring Time

Help colour in our newest
Captain in the Firehouse
(you can also colour-in the title)

Colouring in a drawing in can help you feel relaxed and calm. It's a fun and
easy way to take a break from your worries and focus on the present
moment.

Date _____

Daily MOOd Tracker

This is a chart where you get to track how you're feeling each day. You can tag a smiley face if you're feeling happy, a sad face if you're feeling sad, or a neutral face if you're feeling indifferent. It's a fun way to see how your mood changes over time!

Excited☐　Happy☐　Relaxed☐　Sad☐　Nervous☐　Stressed☐　Angry☐

Creative Visualization Exercise

Have you ever felt really happy and comfortable somewhere special, like your favorite park or your grandparent's house? Well, did you know that you can use your imagination to go there whenever you want?

Here's an exercise to try:
> First, find a quiet and cozy spot where you feel comfortable.
> Then, take a few deep breaths and imagine yourself in your happy place.
> Picture all the details in your mind - what you see, hear, and feel. Imagine you're playing or relaxing there, and try to feel how happy and calm you are.

You can do this exercise whenever you feel worried or scared, or just when you want to feel happy and calm. It's like using your imagination to take a little vacation in your mind!

THE MAZE

When you're solving a maze puzzle, you have to pay attention to where you're going and think about the best way to get to the end. This helps you practice being focused and patient, which are important skills for many things in life. It's also a great way to take a break from your worries and just focus on the puzzle for a little while. When you finish the puzzle, you can feel proud of yourself for working hard and using your brain!

Find a way to piglet and then show him the way out

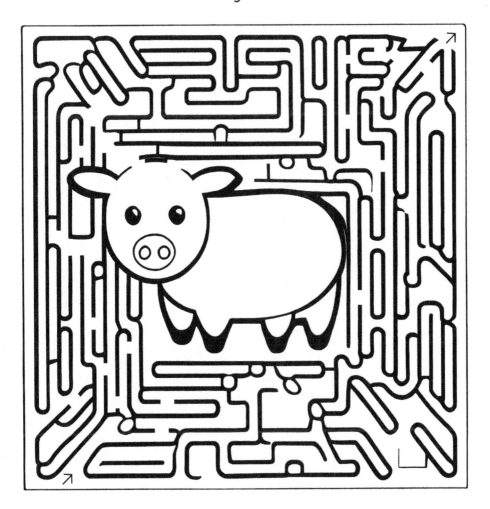

Date _____

Daily Mood Tracker

This is a chart where you get to track how you're feeling each day. You can tag a smiley face if you're feeling happy, a sad face if you're feeling sad, or a neutral face if you're feeling indifferent. It's a fun way to see how your mood changes over time!

 Excited ☐   Happy ☐   Relaxed ☐   Sad ☐   Nervous ☐   Stressed ☐   Angry ☐

Cooking Time

When you follow a recipe, you get to learn about different ingredients and how they work together to make yummy foods. It's like a science experiment!

Cooking and following a recipe can also help you be more mindful. That means that you can focus on what you're doing right now and not worry about other things. You can feel really proud of yourself when you finish making your recipe and see how it turned out! Plus, when you eat what you made, it can make you feel happy and satisfied.

So remember, cooking is not only fun, but it's also a great way to learn and be mindful. You get to try new things and make delicious food that makes you feel happy!

Note for Mum and Dad - Alergies / Intolerances - Food Replacements

cow's milk > almond milk, coconut milk, soy milk, oat milk, rice milk

eggs > mashed bananas, applesauce, silken tofu, vinegar + baking powder

peanuts > sunflower seed butter, soy nut butter, tahini (sesame seed paste)

tree nuts > nut-free butters, such as sunflower seed butter or soy nut butter

soy > coconut milk, almond milk, oat milk, hemp milk

wheat > gluten-free flours, such as rice flour, corn flour, or chickpea flour

fish > tofu, tempeh, beans, lentils, nuts, seeds

shellfish > plant-based proteins, such as tofu, tempeh, beans, lentils, nuts, seeds

sesame > sunflower seeds, pumpkin seeds, flax seeds, chia seeds.

Lets Cook

Baked Oatmeal Cups

Shopping List

- rolled oats ☐
- milk ☐
- eggs ☐
- maple syrup ☐
- baking powder ☐
- cinnamon ☐
- salt ☐
- mixed berries or other fruit ☐
- nuts (optional) ☐

How to

Ingredients:
- 1 1/2 cups rolled oats
- 1/2 cup milk
- 1 egg
- 1/4 cup maple syrup
- 1 teaspoon baking powder
- 1/2 teaspoon cinnamon
- 1/2 teaspoon salt
- 1/2 cup mixed berries or other fruit
- 1/4 cup chopped nuts (optional)

Instructions:
1. Preheat oven to 375°F (190°C). Line a muffin tin with paper liners.
2. In a large mixing bowl, mix together the oats, milk, egg, maple syrup, baking powder, cinnamon, and salt until well combined.
3. Stir in the mixed berries or other fruit, and chopped nuts if using.
4. Spoon the mixture into the prepared muffin tin, filling each cup about 3/4 full.
5. Bake for 25-30 minutes, or until the oatmeal cups are golden brown and set.
6. Allow to cool for a few minutes before serving. Enjoy!

Date _____

Daily Mood Tracker

This is a chart where you get to track how you're feeling each day. You can tag a smiley face if you're feeling happy, a sad face if you're feeling sad, or a neutral face if you're feeling indifferent. It's a fun way to see how your mood changes over time!

Excited ☐   Happy ☐   Relaxed ☐   Sad ☐   Nervous ☐   Stressed ☐   Angry ☐

Daily Affirmations

Read Out Loud

I am confident and capable
I am strong and brave
I am loved and worthy

Repeating affirmations like the ones you just read can make you feel really good inside! It's like saying nice things to yourself that help you feel happy and strong.

You might want to say these affirmations every day, like when waking up in the morning or before you go to bed at night. Or if you don't feel like saying them all the time, you might say them only when you need to feel better, like when you're feeling scared or sad.

It's up to you to decide how often you want to say these affirmations. What's most important is that you believe in the nice things you're saying to yourself and that they help you feel good inside.

So, remember: saying nice things to yourself is a great way to feel confident, strong, and loved!

VISION BOARD

Shopping List

Postcard Paper ☐
Old magazines and Newspapers ☐
Scissors* ☐
Glue ☐
Colouring Pens/Pencils ☐

*always ask for an adult to help you when using scissors

Remember your daily affirmations? Today you are going to build a vision board of your affirmations..

A vision board is like a big piece of paper where you put pictures, words, and things that you really like or that you want to have or do. It's like a giant collage that shows all the things you're dreaming about!

You can hang it up in your room where you can see it every day, to remind you of how confident, strong, brave, loved, and worthy you are!

I am confident and capable

Find pictures of people doing things you would like to learn or try, like playing a new sport or learning an instrument.
Look for images of things that make you happy, like cute animals or fun places to visit.
Cut out words or quotes that inspire you or make you feel good about yourself.

I am strong and brave

Find pictures of people who look strong and confident, like superheroes or athletes.
Look for images of animals that are known for being brave or powerful, like lions or bears.
Cut out words or quotes that remind you to be brave and strong, like "never give up" or "you can do it!"

I am loved and worthy

Find pictures of people who look happy and loved, like families or friends hugging.
Look for images of things that remind you of how special you are, like stars or hearts.
Cut out words or quotes that make you feel loved and important, like "you are amazing" or "you are loved."

Date _____

Daily Mood Tracker

This is a chart where you get to track how you're feeling each day. You can tag a smiley face if you're feeling happy, a sad face if you're feeling sad, or a neutral face if you're feeling indifferent. It's a fun way to see how your mood changes over time!

Excited ☐   Happy ☐   Relaxed ☐   Sad ☐   Nervous ☐   Stressed ☐   Angry ☐

Mindful Meditation

Guided meditation is a really cool way to practice mindfulness! When we meditate, we take a break from all the busy things around us and focus on our breathing and our thoughts. It's like taking a little break for our brains! Guided meditation is when someone talks to us while we meditate so don't forget to ask a parent, sibling or friend to help you.

Focusing on your breathing and counting 1...2...3...each inhale and exhale

Close your eyes and imagine a warm light surrounding your body, giving you a sense of comfort and peace

Imagine yourself in a peaceful place, like a beach or a forest, and listen to the sounds around you

Guides Notes

For children, it's often best to start with shorter meditation sessions and gradually increase the length as they become more comfortable with the practice. A good starting point for younger children might be just a few minutes per day, gradually increasing to 10-15 minutes as they become more comfortable with the practice.

It's important to remember that the quality of the meditation is more important than the quantity of time spent meditating. Even a short session of just a few minutes can be beneficial if it allows the child to focus their attention, calm their mind, and become more aware of their thoughts and feelings.

Nature Walk

Mindfulness is a special way of paying attention to things around us. When we are mindful, we take time to notice what's going on inside our bodies and what's happening in the world around us. Walking in nature is a really great way to practice mindfulness!

When we walk in nature, we get to see so many amazing things - like big trees, colorful flowers, and little animals! We can use all of our senses to experience nature: we can smell the fresh air, feel the soft grass under our feet, hear the birds singing, and even taste the fresh berries growing on the bushes!

Practicing mindfulness while we walk in nature helps us to be more present in the moment. We can take time to really look at and appreciate all the beauty around us. It can also help us feel calm and relaxed. Sometimes, when we are feeling upset or worried, walking in nature can help us feel better!

So, remember: going for a walk in nature and practicing mindfulness is a great way to feel more peaceful and happy. It's a chance to take a break from our busy lives and enjoy the beauty of the world around us.

Write a few words of what you saw and felt during your nature walk.

_____

_____

_____

_____

_____

_____

_____

Date _____

Daily Mood Tracker

This is a chart where you get to track how you're feeling each day. You can tag a smiley face if you're feeling happy, a sad face if you're feeling sad, or a neutral face if you're feeling indifferent. It's a fun way to see how your mood changes over time!

 Excited ☐   Happy ☐   Relaxed ☐   Sad ☐   Nervous ☐   Stressed ☐   Angry ☐

Future Me

Writing a letter to your future self is like talking to yourself in the future! It's a way to imagine what your life might be like when you're older and think about all the things you want to do and be.

Writing a letter to your future self is a good idea for mindfulness because it helps you think about all the things you're grateful for in your life and all the things you hope to achieve. It also helps you focus on the present moment, because you're taking time to think about how you feel right now and how you want to feel in the future.

When you write a letter to your future self, it's a good idea to talk about all the things you like about yourself now and all the things you're proud of. You can also talk about all the things you hope to do or be in the future.

When you're finished writing your letter, you can put it away and read it again in the future! It's a great way to see how much you've grown and changed over time, and to remember all the things you wanted to do and be when you were younger.

Dear future me,

Date _____

Daily Mood Tracker

This is a chart where you get to track how you're feeling each day. You can tag a smiley face if you're feeling happy, a sad face if you're feeling sad, or a neutral face if you're feeling indifferent. It's a fun way to see how your mood changes over time!

Excited ☐   Happy ☐   Relaxed ☐   Sad ☐   Nervous ☐   Stressed ☐   Angry ☐

Gratitude Jar

A gratitude jar or list is like a special place where you can write down all the things that make you happy or that you're grateful for. It's a way to remember all the good things in your life!

When we focus on the things we're grateful for, it helps us feel happier and more positive. It can also help us feel more calm and peaceful. When we write down things we're grateful for, it helps us remember all the good things in our life and not just the things that might be bothering us.

Having a gratitude jar or list is a good idea for mindfulness and mental well-being because it helps us focus on the present moment and appreciate all the good things around us. It also helps us feel more connected to others, because we might write down things we're grateful for about our family and friends.

So, remember: having a gratitude jar or list is a great way to focus on all the good things in our life and feel happier and more positive!

Ready to build your own? Let's do it!

Gratitude Jar

Shopping List

Big Jar ☐
Colouring pens / pencils ☐
Blank paper ☐

Optional Items
Scissors / Old managzines and
newspapers / Old comics / Glue ☐

*always ask for an adult to help you when using scissors

The goal of a gratitude jar is to focus on the positive things in your life and practice gratitude every day. You can write down whatever makes you happy, and put it in the jar to remind you of all the good things in your life!

You can decorate your jar with the optional items in the shopping list and make the jar look good. This is also a good optional activity that will make you feel a sense of accomplishment once you have completed it.

What to put in the jar

There are many things you can put in the jar to show what you are grateful for. Here are a few examples you can use:

Write something about a kind gesture or compliment someone gave you
A happy memory from the day
Something you accomplished or achieved
A favorite quote or inspiring message
A funny moment or joke that made you laugh
A positive affirmation or reminder of your strengths
Something new you learned or discovered
A beautiful sunset or scenery that you saw, either a photo or a drawing
A special moment with a friend or family member
Something you are grateful for, like your health, home, or pets

Remember to include anything that makes you feel happy, thankful, or appreciative. It's a great way to focus on the positive things in your life and to remind yourself of all the good things that you have.

Date _____

Daily MOOd Tracker

This is a chart where you get to track how you're feeling each day. You can tag a smiley face if you're feeling happy, a sad face if you're feeling sad, or a neutral face if you're feeling indifferent. It's a fun way to see how your mood changes over time!

Excited☐   Happy☐   Relaxed☐   Sad☐   Nervous☐   Stressed☐   Angry☐

Self-reflection

Take some time to think about how you're feeling and what's been going on in your life. Ask yourself "why did I tag myself with this emotion?", and write down your answer below.

_____
_____
_____
_____
_____
_____
_____
_____
_____
_____
_____
_____
_____
_____
_____
_____
_____
_____

Colouring Time

Help colour in Sheriff Rex
(you can also colour-in the title)

Date _____

Daily Mood Tracker

This is a chart where you get to track how you're feeling each day. You can tag a smiley face if you're feeling happy, a sad face if you're feeling sad, or a neutral face if you're feeling indifferent. It's a fun way to see how your mood changes over time!

Excited☐   Happy☐   Relaxed☐   Sad☐   Nervous☐   Stressed☐   Angry☐

Mindful Movement

Mindful movement exercises are a fun and healthy way to practice mindfulness. These exercises help us pay attention to our bodies and focus on the present moment.

Some examples of mindful movement exercises include yoga, stretching, and dancing. These exercises are not only fun and enjoyable, but they also help us feel calm and relaxed. When we do these exercises, we breathe deeply and pay attention to the sensations in our body.

For example, when we do yoga, we might move our bodies into different poses while focusing on our breath. We might stretch our arms up to the sky, then slowly reach down to touch our toes. Or we might balance on one foot while focusing on a spot in front of us. These exercises help us focus on the present moment and feel more calm and centered.

Overall, mindful movement exercises are a great way to take care of our bodies and minds. They help us feel more relaxed and present in the moment, and they are also a lot of fun!

Mindful Movement
Exercises

Simple Pose

This pose helps you feel calm and focused. Sit cross-legged on the ground, with your hands on your knees or in your lap. Close your eyes and take a few deep breaths. You can imagine yourself in a peaceful place, like a forest or a beach.

Downward Dog

This pose stretches your arms, shoulders, and legs, and can help you feel more energized. To do it, start on your hands and knees, with your hands under your shoulders and your knees under your hips. Then, lift your hips up and back, straightening your legs and arms. Your body should look like an upside-down "V." Take a few deep breaths, and then come back down to your hands and knees.

Warrior II Pose

This pose helps you feel strong and confident, like a warrior! Start by standing up straight with your feet wide apart. Turn your right foot out to the side, and your left foot in slightly. Raise your arms up to shoulder height, with your palms facing down. Bend your right knee, keeping it over your ankle, and look over your right hand. Take a few deep breaths, and then switch sides.

Remember, yoga is a fun way to move your body while also feeling calm and focused. You can do these exercises whenever you want, and even make up your own poses! Just remember to breathe deeply and listen to your body.

Date _____

Daily MOOd Tracker

This is a chart where you get to track how you're feeling each day. You can tag a smiley face if you're feeling happy, a sad face if you're feeling sad, or a neutral face if you're feeling indifferent. It's a fun way to see how your mood changes over time!

Excited ☐   Happy ☐   Relaxed ☐   Sad ☐   Nervous ☐   Stressed ☐   Angry ☐

Daily Affirmations

Read Out Loud

I am kind and caring to others
I can do my best every day
I am a good friend and listener

Repeating affirmations like the ones you just read can make you feel really good inside! It's like saying nice things to yourself that help you feel happy and strong.

You might want to say these affirmations every day, like when waking up in the morning or before you go to bed at night. Or if you don't feel like saying them all the time, you might say them only when you need to feel better, like when you're feeling scared or sad.

It's up to you to decide how often you want to say these affirmations. What's most important is that you believe in the nice things you're saying to yourself and that they help you feel good inside.

So, remember: saying nice things to yourself is a great way to feel confident, strong, and loved!

THE MAZE

Heelp Vera find her lost friend

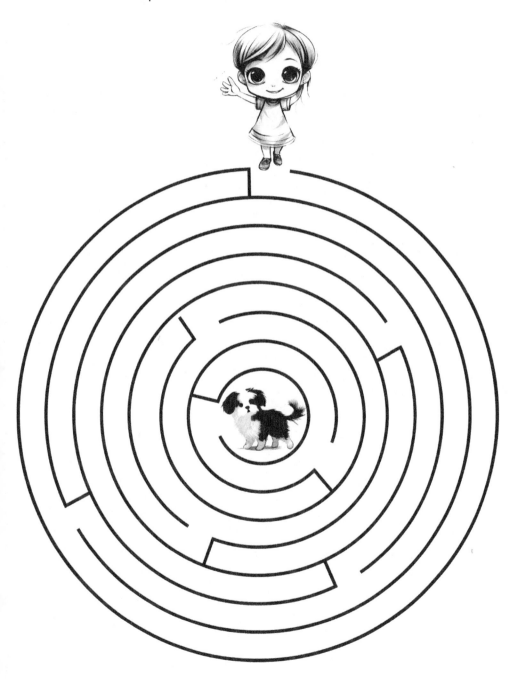

Date _____

Daily MOOd Tracker

This is a chart where you get to track how you're feeling each day. You can tag a smiley face if you're feeling happy, a sad face if you're feeling sad, or a neutral face if you're feeling indifferent. It's a fun way to see how your mood changes over time!

Excited ☐   Happy ☐   Relaxed ☐   Sad ☐   Nervous ☐   Stressed ☐   Angry ☐

Self-reflection

Take some time to think about how you're feeling and what's been going on in your life. Ask yourself "why did I tag myself with this emotion?", and write down your answer below.

_____
_____
_____
_____
_____
_____
_____
_____
_____
_____
_____
_____
_____
_____
_____
_____
_____
_____
_____
_____
_____
_____

Lets Cook

Peanut Butter & Jelly Muffins

Shopping List

Salt ☐
Sugar ☐
Egg ☐
Milk ☐

All-purpose flour ☐
Baking powder ☐
Creamy peanut butter ☐
Vanilla extract ☐
Jelly or Jam (your choice of flavor) ☐

How to

Ingredients:
- 2 cups all-purpose flour
- 2 teaspoons baking powder
- 1/2 teaspoon salt
- 1/2 cup creamy peanut butter
- 1/2 cup sugar
- 1 egg
- 1/2 cup milk
- 1/2 teaspoon vanilla extract
- 1/2 cup jelly or jam (your choice of flavor)

1. Preheat oven to 400°F (200°C). Line a muffin tin with paper liners.
2. In a medium mixing bowl, mix together the flour, baking powder, and salt.
3. In a large mixing bowl, cream together the peanut butter and sugar until light and fluffy.
4. Beat in the egg, followed by the milk and vanilla extract.
5. Gradually add in the dry ingredients, mixing until just combined.
6. Spoon about 1 tablespoon of batter into each muffin cup. Spoon about 1 teaspoon of jelly or jam into the center of each muffin cup. Spoon another tablespoon of batter over the jelly to cover.
7. Bake for 18-20 minutes, or until the muffins are golden brown and a toothpick inserted into the center of a muffin comes out clean.
8. Allow to cool for a few minutes before serving. Enjoy!

Date _____

Daily Mood Tracker

This is a chart where you get to track how you're feeling each day. You can tag a smiley face if you're feeling happy, a sad face if you're feeling sad, or a neutral face if you're feeling indifferent. It's a fun way to see how your mood changes over time!

Excited☐   Happy☐   Relaxed☐   Sad☐   Nervous☐   Stressed☐   Angry☐

Creative Visualization Exercise

Have you ever felt really happy and comfortable somewhere special, like your favorite park or your grandparent's house? Well, did you know that you can use your imagination to go there whenever you want?

Imagine Your Happy Place:
Close your eyes and imagine a place where you feel happy and safe. It could be a beach, a forest, or even your own bedroom. Picture all the details, like the colors, sounds, and smells. Take a few deep breaths and feel the happiness wash over you.

Creative visualization exercises can help you use your imagination and feel calm and happy. Take a deep breath, close your eyes, and let your mind go on a fun adventure!

Dreaming

Keeping a dream journal can be a fun and helpful way to remember your dreams and understand what they might mean. You might even come up with some creative ideas for stories or drawings from your dreams! It's a great idea to write down your dreams in your mindfulness journal, so you can look back on them later and remember all the cool things you dreamed about.

Before you go to sleep, you can think about what you want to dream about, and then when you wake up, you can write down what you remember. You can draw pictures, use stickers, or write down your dreams in words. This can be a fun way to explore your imagination and remember your dreams. Plus, it can help you to understand your thoughts and feelings better. You can also look back at your dream journal and see if there are any patterns or themes in your dreams.

Thoughts before sleep

_____
_____
_____

Emotions before sleep

_____

Dream

_____
_____
_____
_____
_____
_____
_____
_____

Emotions after waking up from the dream

_____

Date _____

Daily Mood Tracker

This is a chart where you get to track how you're feeling each day. You can tag a smiley face if you're feeling happy, a sad face if you're feeling sad, or a neutral face if you're feeling indifferent. It's a fun way to see how your mood changes over time!

Excited ☐   Happy ☐   Relaxed ☐   Sad ☐   Nervous ☐   Stressed ☐   Angry ☐

Goal Setting

Goal setting means deciding what you want to achieve or accomplish in the future, and then figuring out how to make it happen. It's like making a plan or a map to help you get where you want to go. It can be small things like learning to ride a bike or bigger things like getting better grades in school.

When you set a goal, you have something to work towards, and it helps you stay focused and motivated. It can also give you a sense of accomplishment and make you feel proud of yourself when you reach your goal. Goal setting is an important skill to learn because it can help you be successful in many areas of your life, and it can help you develop good habits like planning, organization, and hard work.

Goal Setting

10 types of goal settings that you can work towards

Learning a new skill: You can set a goal to learn a new skill, like how to draw, play an instrument, or ride a bike.

Completing a project: You can set a goal to finish a project you've been working on, like a painting, a puzzle, or a Lego creation.

Reading a certain number of books: You can set a goal to read a certain number of books in a month or a year, and track your progress in a journal (like this one)

Trying new foods: You can set a goal to try new foods, like different fruits or vegetables, and keep track of your favorites.

Making new friends: You can set a goal to make new friends, and think about ways you can be kind and helpful to others.

Practicing kindness: You can set a goal to practice kindness every day, like saying thank you, helping someone in need, or giving a compliment.

Keeping a tidy room: You can set a goal to keep your room clean and organized, and think of ways to make it fun, like decorating with posters or stickers.

Being more mindful: You can set a goal to be more mindful, like taking deep breaths when you feel upset, or focusing on the present moment instead of worrying about the past or future.

Getting exercise: You can set a goal to get exercise every day, like going for a walk, riding a bike, or playing a sport.

Trying new activities: You can set a goal to try new activities, like visiting a new place, learning a new game, or trying a new hobby.

Write a list of goals you would like to start with.
I will remind you once and a while thoughout this journal for you to write down more goals and how the ones you have picked originally are going.

Date _____

Daily MOOd Tracker

This is a chart where you get to track how you're feeling each day. You can tag a smiley face if you're feeling happy, a sad face if you're feeling sad, or a neutral face if you're feeling indifferent. It's a fun way to see how your mood changes over time!

Excited☐   Happy☐   Relaxed☐   Sad☐   Nervous☐   Stressed☐   Angry☐

DIY

What? DIY? Don't worry, it's not as complicated as it sounds! DIY stands for "Do It Yourself" and it means making things with your own hands, instead of buying them from a store.

Doing DIY projects can be a great way to practice mindfulness and boost creativity. When you make something with your own hands, you get a sense of satisfaction and accomplishment that you can't get from buying something ready-made. Plus, when you're focused on creating something, it can help you stay present in the moment and forget about any worries or stress you might be feeling. And the best part is, there are so many things you can make! You can build a birdhouse for your backyard, decorate a plant pot for your room, or even make your own jewelry. The possibilities are endless! So, next time you're feeling bored or stressed, try a DIY project and see how it makes you feel.

Vase and Water Tray

Materials:
Molding clay

1. Roll a clay ball with your hands until it's about the size of your fist.

2. Use your thumb and fingers to pinch the clay ball from the top to the bottom, creating a pot shape.

3. Keep the walls of the pot even in thickness. Smooth the inside and outside of the pot using a damp sponge or your fingers.

4. Use a wooden stick or other tool to make drainage holes at the bottom of the pot.

5. Let the pot dry for a few hours until it's firm to the touch.

Once the pot is dry, paint or decorate it with markers. You can also use clay to make designs or shapes to stick onto the pot.
Let the paint or decorations dry completely.
You can also use the same technique to create a water collection tray as shown on the right (you don't want to damageyour floor with water stains).

Date _____

Daily MOOd Tracker

This is a chart where you get to track how you're feeling each day. You can tag a smiley face if you're feeling happy, a sad face if you're feeling sad, or a neutral face if you're feeling indifferent. It's a fun way to see how your mood changes over time!

Excited☐ Happy☐ Relaxed☐ Sad☐ Nervous☐ Stressed☐ Angry☐

GratitUde Jar

Don't forget to add to your Gratitude Jar!
Remember that your gratitude jar is that jar that you can fill with notes about things that you are thankful for or that make you happy. It's important because when we focus on the good things in our life, we feel happier and more content. Plus, it's a fun way to remember all the wonderful things that happen to us every day, even the small things that we might forget about otherwise.

Colouring Time

Help colour in Brocolli the Smiler
(you can also colour-in the title)

Date _____

Daily Mood Tracker

This is a chart where you get to track how you're feeling each day. You can tag a smiley face if you're feeling happy, a sad face if you're feeling sad, or a neutral face if you're feeling indifferent. It's a fun way to see how your mood changes over time!

Excited ☐   Happy ☐   Relaxed ☐   Sad ☐   Nervous ☐   Stressed ☐   Angry ☐

Daily Affirmations

Read Out Loud

I am always learning and evolving each day
I am enveloped by affection and encouragement
I am liberated from worry, fear, and negativity

Repeating affirmations like the ones you just read can make you feel really good inside! It's like saying nice things to yourself that help you feel happy and strong.

You might want to say these affirmations every day, like when waking up in the morning or before you go to bed at night. Or if you don't feel like saying them all the time, you might say them only when you need to feel better, like when you're feeling scared or sad.

It's up to you to decide how often you want to say these affirmations. What's most important is that you believe in the nice things you're saying to yourself and that they help you feel good inside.

So, remember: saying nice things to yourself is a great way to feel confident, strong, and loved!

Dreaming

Believe in your dreams and they may come true. Believe in yourself and they will come true.

Thoughts before sleep

_____
_____
_____

Emotions before sleep

_____

Dream

_____
_____
_____
_____
_____
_____
_____
_____
_____
_____
_____
_____
_____
_____

Emotions after waking up from the dream

_____

Date _____

Daily Mood Tracker

This is a chart where you get to track how you're feeling each day. You can tag a smiley face if you're feeling happy, a sad face if you're feeling sad, or a neutral face if you're feeling indifferent. It's a fun way to see how your mood changes over time!

Excited ☐   Happy ☐   Relaxed ☐   Sad ☐   Nervous ☐   Stressed ☐   Angry ☐

Mindful Meditation

Guided meditation is a really cool way to practice mindfulness! When we meditate, we take a break from all the busy things around us and focus on our breathing and our thoughts. It's like taking a little break for our brains! Guided meditation is when someone talks to us while we meditate so don't forget to ask a parent, sibling or friend to help you.

Focusing on your breathing and counting 1...2....3...each inhale and exhale

Close your eyes and imagine a warm light surrounding your body, giving you a sense of comfort and peace

Imagine yourself in a peaceful place, like a beach or a forest, and listen to the sounds around you

Guides Notes

For children, it's often best to start with shorter meditation sessions and gradually increase the length as they become more comfortable with the practice. A good starting point for younger children might be just a few minutes per day, gradually increasing to 10-15 minutes as they become more comfortable with the practice.

It's important to remember that the quality of the meditation is more important than the quantity of time spent meditating. Even a short session of just a few minutes can be beneficial if it allows the child to focus their attention, calm their mind, and become more aware of their thoughts and feelings.

Nature Walk

Mindfulness is a special way of paying attention to things around us. When we are mindful, we take time to notice what's going on inside our bodies and what's happening in the world around us. Walking in nature is a really great way to practice mindfulness!

When we walk in nature, we get to see so many amazing things - like big trees, colorful flowers, and little animals! We can use all of our senses to experience nature: we can smell the fresh air, feel the soft grass under our feet, hear the birds singing, and even taste the fresh berries growing on the bushes!

Practicing mindfulness while we walk in nature helps us to be more present in the moment. We can take time to really look at and appreciate all the beauty around us. It can also help us feel calm and relaxed. Sometimes, when we are feeling upset or worried, walking in nature can help us feel better!

Write a few words of what you saw and felt during your nature walk.

_____

_____

_____

_____

_____

_____

_____

_____

_____

_____

Date _____

Daily Mood Tracker

This is a chart where you get to track how you're feeling each day. You can tag a smiley face if you're feeling happy, a sad face if you're feeling sad, or a neutral face if you're feeling indifferent. It's a fun way to see how your mood changes over time!

Excited ☐   Happy ☐   Relaxed ☐   Sad ☐   Nervous ☐   Stressed ☐   Angry ☐

Mindful Photography

Have you ever used a camera to take pictures? It's really fun! Mindful photography is when you use your camera to take pictures of things that make you feel happy or calm. You can go outside and take pictures of nature, like trees and flowers, or maybe you want to take pictures of your favorite toys or your family and friends.

After you take your pictures, you can look at them and think about how you felt when you took them. Maybe you felt really happy when you took a picture of a pretty flower, or maybe you felt calm when you took a picture of a peaceful sunset. Mindful photography helps you focus on the good things in life and remember how you felt in those happy or calm moments.

THE MAZE

Find a way to guide our friend to her flower
so she can water it

Date _____

Daily Mood Tracker

This is a chart where you get to track how you're feeling each day. You can tag a smiley face if you're feeling happy, a sad face if you're feeling sad, or a neutral face if you're feeling indifferent. It's a fun way to see how your mood changes over time!

 Excited☐ Happy☐ Relaxed☐ Sad☐ Nervous☐ Stressed☐ Angry☐

Mindful Music

Have you ever listened to music and felt really happy or relaxed? Well, that's because music can be a really great way to calm your mind and body. When we listen to calm music, it helps us to focus our attention and feel more relaxed.

So, for this activity, we're going to practice being mindful with music. You can listen to different kinds of music and see which ones make you feel relaxed and happy. You can even create your own music if you'd like!

Just find a quiet place where you can listen to music without any distractions. Sit down, take a deep breath, and listen to the music. Focus on the different sounds and instruments you can hear. Pay attention to how the music makes you feel.

This is a great way to practice mindfulness and relaxation, and it's really fun too!

Lets Cook

Veggie Quesadillas

Shopping List

Whole wheat tortillas ☐
Shredded cheese ☐
Olive oil ☐
Diced vegetables* ☐

*these can be what you prefer, onion, courgette, mushrooms, bell peppers, brocolli, carrots, etc

How to

Ingredients:
• 4 whole wheat tortillas
• 1 cup shredded cheese
• 1 cup diced vegetables
• 1 tablespoon olive oil

1. Heat a large skillet over medium heat.
2. Place a tortilla on the skillet.
3. Sprinkle shredded cheese and diced vegetables on half of the tortilla.
4. Fold the tortilla in half, covering the cheese and veggies.
5. Brush the top with olive oil.
6. Cook for 2-3 minutes on each side or until cheese is melted and the tortilla is crispy and golden.
7. Repeat the steps for the remaining tortillas.
8. Cut each quesadilla into wedges and serve hot with a optional side of salsa or guacamole.

Date _____

Daily Mood Tracker

This is a chart where you get to track how you're feeling each day. You can tag a smiley face if you're feeling happy, a sad face if you're feeling sad, or a neutral face if you're feeling indifferent. It's a fun way to see how your mood changes over time!

 Excited ☐ Happy ☐ Relaxed ☐ Sad ☐ Nervous ☐ Stressed ☐ Angry ☐

Mindful Breathing

I'm going to teach you about Mindful Breathing Games! They're games that can help you relax and focus on your breath. For "Blow Out the Candle," you can pretend to hold a candle and blow it out slowly while taking a deep breath in and then breathing out slowly. You can repeat this game a few times and focus on your breath and the feeling of blowing out the candle.

Mindful Movement
Exercises

Cat Pose

This pose stretches your back and helps you feel more flexible. Start on your hands and knees, with your hands under your shoulders and your knees under your hips. Arch your back up, like a cat stretching, and lower your head down. Take a few deep breaths, and then come back to a flat back.

Tree Pose

This pose helps you feel grounded and balanced. Stand up straight with your feet together. Put one foot on the inside of the opposite leg, above or below the knee. Bring your hands together in front of your chest, like you're praying. Take a few deep breaths, and then switch sides.

Warrior Pose

This pose helps you feel strong and powerful, like a warrior! Start by standing up straight with your feet hip-distance apart. Step your left foot back behind you, and turn it out slightly. Bend your right knee, keeping it over your ankle. Raise your arms up above your head, with your palms together in prayer position. Look up between your hands and take a few deep breaths. Then switch sides and repeat.

Yoga is a great way to move your body and feel calm and focused. You can practice these poses anytime you want and even make up your own poses! It's important to remember to take deep breaths and pay attention to how your body feels. So have fun, be creative, and enjoy the benefits of yoga!

Date _____

Daily Mood Tracker

This is a chart where you get to track how you're feeling each day. You can tag a smiley face if you're feeling happy, a sad face if you're feeling sad, or a neutral face if you're feeling indifferent. It's a fun way to see how your mood changes over time!

Excited☐ Happy☐ Relaxed☐ Sad☐ Nervous☐ Stressed☐ Angry☐

Self-reflection

Take some time to think about how you're feeling and what's been going on in your life. Ask yourself "why did I tag myself with this emotion?", and write down your answer below.

_____
_____
_____
_____
_____
_____
_____
_____
_____
_____
_____
_____
_____
_____
_____
_____
_____
_____
_____
_____
_____

Dreaming

Dreams may seem impossible, but with hard work and determination, they can become a reality.

Thoughts before sleep

_____
_____
_____
_____

Emotions before sleep

_____

Dream

_____
_____
_____
_____
_____
_____
_____
_____
_____
_____
_____
_____
_____
_____
_____
_____

Emotions after waking up from the dream

_____

Date _____

Daily Mood Tracker

This is a chart where you get to track how you're feeling each day. You can tag a smiley face if you're feeling happy, a sad face if you're feeling sad, or a neutral face if you're feeling indifferent. It's a fun way to see how your mood changes over time!

Excited ☐   Happy ☐   Relaxed ☐   Sad ☐   Nervous ☐   Stressed ☐   Angry ☐

Daily Affirmations
Read Out Loud

I am brimming with hope and positivity
I believe in my skills and choices
I am thankful for the wonders in my life

Daily affirmations are like little pep talks we give ourselves. When we say nice things about ourselves, it helps us feel happier and more confident. This is really important for children because it helps us grow up to be strong and brave.

You might want to say these affirmations every day, like when waking up in the morning or before you go to bed at night. Or if you don't feel like saying them all the time, you might say them only when you need to feel better, like when you're feeling scared or sad.

It's up to you to decide how often you want to say these affirmations. What's most important is that you believe in the nice things you're saying to yourself and that they help you feel good inside.

So, remember: saying nice things to yourself is a great way to feel confident, strong, and loved!

Colouring Time

Help colour in the Carrot Amazon
(you can also colour-in the title)

Date _____

Daily MOOd Tracker

This is a chart where you get to track how you're feeling each day. You can tag a smiley face if you're feeling happy, a sad face if you're feeling sad, or a neutral face if you're feeling indifferent. It's a fun way to see how your mood changes over time!

Excited ☐   Happy ☐   Relaxed ☐   Sad ☐   Nervous ☐   Stressed ☐   Angry ☐

Mindful Meditation

Guided meditation is a really cool way to practice mindfulness! When we meditate, we take a break from all the busy things around us and focus on our breathing and our thoughts. It's like taking a little break for our brains! Guided meditation is when someone talks to us while we meditate so don't forget to ask a parent, sibling or friend to help you.

Focusing on your breathing and counting 1...2....3...each inhale and exhale

Close your eyes and imagine a warm light surrounding your body, giving you a sense of comfort and peace

Imagine yourself in a peaceful place, like a beach or a forest, and listen to the sounds around you

Guides Notes

For children, it's often best to start with shorter meditation sessions and gradually increase the length as they become more comfortable with the practice. A good starting point for younger children might be just a few minutes per day, gradually increasing to 10-15 minutes as they become more comfortable with the practice.

It's important to remember that the quality of the meditation is more important than the quantity of time spent meditating. Even a short session of just a few minutes can be beneficial if it allows the child to focus their attention, calm their mind, and become more aware of their thoughts and feelings.

Nature Walk

Mindfulness is a special way of paying attention to things around us. When we are mindful, we take time to notice what's going on inside our bodies and what's happening in the world around us. Walking in nature is a really great way to practice mindfulness!

When we walk in nature, we get to see so many amazing things - like big trees, colorful flowers, and little animals! We can use all of our senses to experience nature: we can smell the fresh air, feel the soft grass under our feet, hear the birds singing, and even taste the fresh berries growing on the bushes!

Write a few words of what you saw and felt during your nature walk.

_____
_____
_____
_____
_____
_____
_____
_____
_____
_____
_____
_____
_____
_____
_____
_____
_____
_____

Date _____

Daily Mood Tracker

This is a chart where you get to track how you're feeling each day. You can tag a smiley face if you're feeling happy, a sad face if you're feeling sad, or a neutral face if you're feeling indifferent. It's a fun way to see how your mood changes over time!

 Excited ☐ Happy ☐ Relaxed ☐ Sad ☐ Nervous ☐ Stressed ☐ Angry ☐

Creative Visualization Exercise

Have you ever felt really happy and comfortable somewhere special, like your favorite park or your grandparent's house? Well, did you know that you can use your imagination to go there whenever you want?

Animal Adventure:
Imagine that you're an animal exploring a new world. Maybe you're a bird flying over the mountains, or a fish swimming in the ocean. Picture all the details, like the scenery, the weather, and the other animals you meet. Feel the excitement of your adventure!

By using your imagination in creative visualization exercises, you can feel happy and relaxed. Take a deep breath, close your eyes, and let your thoughts take you on a fun journey!

Goal Setting

Remember, it's important to choose goals that are achievable and that make you happy. Don't be afraid to set small goals that lead to bigger ones!

Which goals have you set and achieved so far?

_____

_____

_____

_____

_____

_____

_____

How did accomplishing these goals make you feel?

_____

_____

_____

_____

What are some goals that you would like to set for yourself? It could be something you want to learn, a skill you want to improve, or a task you want to complete. Make a list of things you would like to achieve!

☐ _____   ☐ _____

☐ _____   ☐ _____

☐ _____   ☐ _____

☐ _____   ☐ _____

☐ _____   ☐ _____

☐ _____   ☐ _____

☐ _____   ☐ _____

Date _____

Daily Mood Tracker

This is a chart where you get to track how you're feeling each day. You can tag a smiley face if you're feeling happy, a sad face if you're feeling sad, or a neutral face if you're feeling indifferent. It's a fun way to see how your mood changes over time!

Excited ☐   Happy ☐   Relaxed ☐   Sad ☐   Nervous ☐   Stressed ☐   Angry ☐

Bumble Bee Breathing

"Bumble Bee Breathing" is another game where you breathe in deeply and then exhale while making a humming sound like a bumble bee.
You can do this a few times and focus on the feeling of your breath and the sound you're making.

Birdhouse

Materials:

A piece of wood or recycled materials (such as cardboard, plastic bottles, or milk cartons)
A hammer
Nails or screws or glue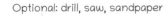
Paint or markers for decorating
Optional: drill, saw, sandpaper

Instructions:

1. Cut the wood or recycled materials to the size you want for your birdhouse.
2. Use the hammer and nails or screws to assemble the birdhouse. You can make a simple box shape or add a sloping roof if you like. Make sure to leave a small hole in the front for the birds to enter.
3. Sand the edges and surfaces of the birdhouse to make it smooth and safe for the birds.
4. Paint or decorate the birdhouse with your own designs. You can use bright colors, patterns, or natural materials like sticks and leaves to make it look like a real bird's nest.
5. Once your birdhouse is finished, find a good spot to hang it outside. Make sure it's in a safe place away from predators and in a location that's attractive to birds.

You can fill it with some straw or twigs to make it cozy for your feathered friends. Enjoy watching the birds come and go from your homemade birdhouse!

Plastic Bottle

Milk carton

Sticks and Glue

Date _____

Daily Mood Tracker

This is a chart where you get to track how you're feeling each day. You can tag a smiley face if you're feeling happy, a sad face if you're feeling sad, or a neutral face if you're feeling indifferent. It's a fun way to see how your mood changes over time!

Excited☐ Happy☐ Relaxed☐ Sad☐ Nervous☐ Stressed☐ Angry☐

Positive Word Search

Hey there! Today, we're going to play a super fun game called "Positive Word Search." It's like a treasure hunt, but instead of looking for hidden treasures, we'll be searching for special words that make us feel happy and good about ourselves. Ready to give it a try?

Here's how it works: You'll get a grid filled with lots of letters, and we've hidden some secret words inside. Your mission is to find these words that are hiding among the other letters. They can be arranged up, down, sideways, or even diagonally! When you spot a word, circle it or highlight it with a cool color.

Kindness
Courage
Joyful
Grateful
Love
Friendship
Creativity
Confidence
Laughter
Generosity

```
K  I  N  D  N  E  S  S  R  T  B  A  E  F
C  O  U  R  A  G  E  Y  J  O  Y  P  L  E
R  E  V  I  T  A  E  R  C  O  U  D  G  M
L  A  U  G  H  T  E  R  F  R  I  E  S  R
A  W  R  O  L  P  X  Y  S  G  H  O  Y  E
O  I  L  E  O  J  V  E  N  Z  M  N  N  V
V  B  F  R  I  E  N  D  S  H  I  P  I  I
G  R  A  T  E  F  U  L  N  E  S  S  U  T
E  L  Y  T  I  V  I  T  A  E  R  C  G  E
C  O  N  F  I  D  E  N  C  E  I  O  R  Y
T  V  Q  W  X  Y  Z  B  A  R  H  G  F  I
L  O  V  E  R  S  T  U  V  W  X  Y  Z  S
M  E  N  O  S  R  E  G  G  E  N  O  R  G
```

 Remember, this game is not just about finding the words, but also about understanding their meanings and how they can bring happiness and positivity to our lives. So put on your word detective hat and get ready for an exciting adventure!

THE MAZE

Take each girl to their respective house

Date _____

Daily MOOd Tracker

This is a chart where you get to track how you're feeling each day. You can tag a smiley face if you're feeling happy, a sad face if you're feeling sad, or a neutral face if you're feeling indifferent. It's a fun way to see how your mood changes over time!

Excited☐ Happy☐ Relaxed☐ Sad☐ Nervous☐ Stressed☐ Angry☐

Balloon Breathing

"Balloon Breathing" is another fun game where you can imagine blowing up a balloon as you inhale, and then letting the air out of the balloon as you exhale. You can do this a few times and focus on the feeling of your breath and the imaginary balloon.

These games can help you learn how to use your breath to feel relaxed, focused, and calm. It's a great way to take a break and feel better when you're feeling stressed or worried.

Lets Cook

Healthy Chicken Nuggets

Shopping List

Basil ☐ Garlic powder ☐
Oregano ☐ Black pepper ☐
Paprika ☐ Olive oil ☐
Salt ☐ Breadcrumbs ☐
Eggs ☐ Chicken breasts ☐

How to

Ingredients:
- 1 pound boneless, skinless chicken breast, cut into bite-sized pieces
- 1 cup whole wheat breadcrumbs
- 1/2 teaspoon dried basil
- 1/2 teaspoon dried oregano
- 1/2 teaspoon garlic powder
- 1/2 teaspoon paprika
- 1/2 teaspoon salt
- 1/4 teaspoon black pepper
- 1 large egg, beaten
- 1 tablespoon olive oil
- Non-stick cooking spray

1. Preheat the oven to 425°F (220°C). Line a large baking sheet with parchment paper and spray with non-stick cooking spray.
2. In a shallow dish, mix together the breadcrumbs, basil, oregano, garlic powder, paprika, salt, and pepper.
3. In another shallow dish, beat the egg.
4. Dip each chicken piece into the beaten egg, then coat in the breadcrumb mixture. Place the coated chicken on the prepared baking sheet.
5. Drizzle the olive oil over the chicken.
6. Bake in the oven for 15-20 minutes, or until the chicken is golden brown and cooked through.
7. Serve with a side of your choice, such as roasted vegetables or a green salad.

Date _____

Daily MOOd Tracker

This is a chart where you get to track how you're feeling each day. You can tag a smiley face if you're feeling happy, a sad face if you're feeling sad, or a neutral face if you're feeling indifferent. It's a fun way to see how your mood changes over time!

 Excited ☐   Happy ☐   Relaxed ☐   Sad ☐   Nervous ☐   Stressed ☐   Angry ☐

Daily Affirmations

Read Out Loud

I am deserving of joy and accomplishment
I can face any obstacle with determination
I am embraced and accepted for who I am

Saying positive things to ourselves can also make it easier for us to make friends. When we believe we are kind and good, other kids will want to be our friends too. Friendships make our lives more fun and exciting!

You might want to say these affirmations every day, like when waking up in the morning or before you go to bed at night. Or if you don't feel like saying them all the time, you might say them only when you need to feel better, like when you're feeling scared or sad.

It's up to you to decide how often you want to say these affirmations. What's most important is that you believe in the nice things you're saying to yourself and that they help you feel good inside.

So, remember: saying nice things to yourself is a great way to feel confident, strong, and loved!

Dreaming

Our dreams are like magic carpets that take us on journeys of discovery and self-discovery.

Thoughts before sleep

_____
_____
_____

Emotions before sleep

_____

Dream

_____
_____
_____
_____
_____
_____
_____
_____
_____
_____
_____
_____
_____
_____
_____

Emotions after waking up from the dream

_____

Date _____

Daily MOOd Tracker

This is a chart where you get to track how you're feeling each day. You can tag a smiley face if you're feeling happy, a sad face if you're feeling sad, or a neutral face if you're feeling indifferent. It's a fun way to see how your mood changes over time!

Excited ☐   Happy ☐   Relaxed ☐   Sad ☐   Nervous ☐   Stressed ☐   Angry ☐

Mindful Meditation

Guided meditation is a really cool way to practice mindfulness! When we meditate, we take a break from all the busy things around us and focus on our breathing and our thoughts. It's like taking a little break for our brains! Guided meditation is when someone talks to us while we meditate so don't forget to ask a parent, sibling or friend to help you.

Focusing on your breathing and counting 1...2....3...each inhale and exhale

Close your eyes and imagine a warm light surrounding your body, giving you a sense of comfort and peace

Imagine yourself in a peaceful place, like a beach or a forest, and listen to the sounds around you

Guides Notes

For children, it's often best to start with shorter meditation sessions and gradually increase the length as they become more comfortable with the practice. A good starting point for younger children might be just a few minutes per day, gradually increasing to 10-15 minutes as they become more comfortable with the practice.

It's important to remember that the quality of the meditation is more important than the quantity of time spent meditating. Even a short session of just a few minutes can be beneficial if it allows the child to focus their attention, calm their mind, and become more aware of their thoughts and feelings.

Colouring Time

Help colour in Lizzy
(you can also colour-in the title)

Date _____

Daily Mood Tracker

This is a chart where you get to track how you're feeling each day. You can tag a smiley face if you're feeling happy, a sad face if you're feeling sad, or a neutral face if you're feeling indifferent. It's a fun way to see how your mood changes over time!

Excited ☐   Happy ☐   Relaxed ☐   Sad ☐   Nervous ☐   Stressed ☐   Angry ☐

Gratitude Jar

Don't forget about your special jar where you can keep little notes about things that make you happy or that you're grateful for. It's important because it helps you focus on the good things in your life, and when you focus on the good, you start to feel happier and more positive. Plus, it's always nice to have a little jar of happy thoughts to turn to when you're feeling sad.

Nature Walk

Mindfulness is a special way of paying attention to things around us. When we are mindful, we take time to notice what's going on inside our bodies and what's happening in the world around us. Walking in nature is a really great way to practice mindfulness!

When we walk in nature, we get to see so many amazing things - like big trees, colorful flowers, and little animals! We can use all of our senses to experience nature: we can smell the fresh air, feel the soft grass under our feet, hear the birds singing, and even taste the fresh berries growing on the bushes!

Write a few words of what you saw and felt during your nature walk.

Date _____

Daily Mood Tracker

This is a chart where you get to track how you're feeling each day. You can tag a smiley face if you're feeling happy, a sad face if you're feeling sad, or a neutral face if you're feeling indifferent. It's a fun way to see how your mood changes over time!

Excited ☐   Happy ☐   Relaxed ☐   Sad ☐   Nervous ☐   Stressed ☐   Angry ☐

Self-reflection

Take some time to think about how you're feeling and what's been going on in your life. Ask yourself "why did I tag myself with this emotion?", and write down your answer below.

_____
_____
_____
_____
_____
_____
_____
_____
_____
_____
_____
_____
_____
_____
_____
_____
_____
_____
_____
_____
_____
_____
_____

Dreaming

Dreams are the sparks that light the fire of our imagination and fuel our passion to succeed.

Thoughts before sleep

_____
_____
_____

Emotions before sleep

_____

Dream

_____
_____
_____
_____
_____
_____
_____
_____
_____
_____
_____
_____
_____
_____

Emotions after waking up from the dream

_____

Date _____

Daily Mood Tracker

This is a chart where you get to track how you're feeling each day. You can tag a smiley face if you're feeling happy, a sad face if you're feeling sad, or a neutral face if you're feeling indifferent. It's a fun way to see how your mood changes over time!

Excited ☐   Happy ☐   Relaxed ☐   Sad ☐   Nervous ☐   Stressed ☐   Angry ☐

I Spy...

Have you ever played "I Spy"? It's a really fun game that can help you practice mindfulness. Here's how it works: one person looks around the room and picks something they see. Then, they say "I spy with my little eye something that is [insert a color or description of the object]."

The other person then has to guess what the object is. But here's the mindful part: before the guesser can answer, they have to take a deep breath and really focus on looking around the room to find the object. This helps them be present in the moment and really pay attention to their surroundings.

Then, the guesser can answer with their guess. The game can go back and forth between players, with each person taking a turn to spy something in the room. It's a fun way to practice mindfulness and really focus on what's around you.

Mindful Movement
Exercises

Butterfly Pose

This pose stretches your hips and inner thighs, and can help you feel more relaxed. Sit on the ground with your knees bent and the soles of your feet touching each other. Hold onto your ankles and gently flap your legs up and down, like a butterfly's wings. Take a few deep breaths, and then relax your legs.

Bridge Pose

This pose strengthens your legs and stretches your back. Lie on your back with your knees bent and your feet flat on the ground. Lift your hips up, so your body makes a straight line from your shoulders to your knees. You can hold onto your ankles or interlace your fingers under your back. Take a few deep breaths, and then lower your hips back down.

Cobra Pose

This pose stretches your chest and back, and can help you feel more confident. Lie on your stomach with your hands under your shoulders. Press your hands into the ground and lift your chest up, keeping your elbows close to your body. Take a few deep breaths, and then lower back down.

Remember, mindful movement exercises are a way to move your body while also focusing on how you're feeling inside. They can help you feel calm, happy, and more aware of your thoughts and emotions!

Date _____

Daily Mood Tracker

This is a chart where you get to track how you're feeling each day. You can tag a smiley face if you're feeling happy, a sad face if you're feeling sad, or a neutral face if you're feeling indifferent. It's a fun way to see how your mood changes over time!

 Excited ☐ Happy ☐ Relaxed ☐ Sad ☐ Nervous ☐ Stressed ☐ Angry ☐

"Five Senses Countdown." This game is all about exploring and paying attention to the world around us using our five senses: sight, touch, hearing, smell, and taste. This activity will help you become more mindful and present in the moment. Are you ready to begin? Let's start by finding a comfortable spot where you can sit or stand while we explore our senses.

First, let's use our sense of sight. Look around and find five things you can see. It could be anything from a colorful flower to a picture on the wall. Take a moment to really observe each item, noticing the colors, shapes, and details. Once you've found five things, move on to touch. Find four things around you that you can touch. Feel the texture of each item and think about whether it's smooth, rough, soft, or hard. As you do this, try to focus on the sensations you feel in your fingertips.

Next, we'll focus on our sense of hearing. Close your eyes and listen carefully to the sounds around you. Can you identify three different sounds? It might be the gentle hum of a fan, the chirping of birds outside, or the distant sound of a car passing by. Now, let's move on to our sense of smell. Take a few deep breaths and try to find two things you can smell. It could be the scent of a freshly baked cookie or the aroma of a flower. Finally, let's use our sense of taste. Find one thing you can taste, like a small piece of fruit or a sip of water. Focus on the flavor as you enjoy it.

By taking the time to notice and appreciate the world around you using all your senses, you've practiced mindfulness. Mindfulness helps us feel more connected and present in our lives.

Goal Setting

Setting goals helps you focus on what you want to achieve in life and gives you a sense of direction.

Which goals have you set and achieved so far?

_____
_____
_____
_____
_____
_____
_____
_____

How did accomplishing these goals make you feel?

_____
_____
_____
_____
_____

What are some goals that you would like to set for yourself? It could be something you want to learn, a skill you want to improve, or a task you want to complete. Make a list of things you would like to achieve!

- ☐ _____   ☐ _____
- ☐ _____   ☐ _____
- ☐ _____   ☐ _____
- ☐ _____   ☐ _____
- ☐ _____   ☐ _____
- ☐ _____   ☐ _____
- ☐ _____   ☐ _____

Date _____

Daily Mood Tracker

This is a chart where you get to track how you're feeling each day. You can tag a smiley face if you're feeling happy, a sad face if you're feeling sad, or a neutral face if you're feeling indifferent. It's a fun way to see how your mood changes over time!

Excited ☐   Happy ☐   Relaxed ☐   Sad ☐   Nervous ☐   Stressed ☐   Angry ☐

Daily Affirmations

Read Out Loud

I am resilient and resourceful
I am courageous and fearless
I am cherished and valued

Affirmations help us believe we can do hard things. Sometimes, we might feel scared or unsure about trying something new. But if we say, "I am brave and strong," it gives us the courage to try new activities and face challenges.

You might want to say these affirmations every day, like when waking up in the morning or before you go to bed at night. Or if you don't feel like saying them all the time, you might say them only when you need to feel better, like when you're feeling scared or sad.

It's up to you to decide how often you want to say these affirmations. What's most important is that you believe in the nice things you're saying to yourself and that they help you feel good inside.

So, remember: saying nice things to yourself is a great way to feel confident, strong, and loved!

THE MAZE

Mr Panda is a bit hungry, why don't you show him the way to the bamboo

Date _____

Daily Mood Tracker

This is a chart where you get to track how you're feeling each day. You can tag a smiley face if you're feeling happy, a sad face if you're feeling sad, or a neutral face if you're feeling indifferent. It's a fun way to see how your mood changes over time!

Excited ☐   Happy ☐   Relaxed ☐   Sad ☐   Nervous ☐   Stressed ☐   Angry ☐

Mindful Meditation

Guided meditation is a really cool way to practice mindfulness! When we meditate, we take a break from all the busy things around us and focus on our breathing and our thoughts. It's like taking a little break for our brains! Guided meditation is when someone talks to us while we meditate so don't forget to ask a parent, sibling or friend to help you.

Focusing on your breathing and counting 1...2....3...each inhale and exhale

Close your eyes and imagine a warm light surrounding your body, giving you a sense of comfort and peace

Imagine yourself in a peaceful place, like a beach or a forest, and listen to the sounds around you

Guides Notes

For children, it's often best to start with shorter meditation sessions and gradually increase the length as they become more comfortable with the practice. A good starting point for younger children might be just a few minutes per day, gradually increasing to 10-15 minutes as they become more comfortable with the practice.

It's important to remember that the quality of the meditation is more important than the quantity of time spent meditating. Even a short session of just a few minutes can be beneficial if it allows the child to focus their attention, calm their mind, and become more aware of their thoughts and feelings.

Lets Cook

Sweet Potato Fries

Shopping List

Sweet potatoes ☐
Black pepper ☐
Paprika ☐
Olive oil ☐
Salt ☐

How to

Ingredients:
• 2 medium sweet potatoes, peeled and sliced into fries
• 2 tablespoons olive oil
• 1 teaspoon salt
• 1 teaspoon black pepper
• 1 teaspoon paprika

1. Preheat the oven to 400°F.
2. Line a baking sheet with parchment paper.
3. In a large bowl, mix together the sliced sweet potatoes, olive oil, salt, black pepper, and paprika.
4. Spread the sweet potatoes evenly on the prepared baking sheet.
5. Bake for 25-30 minutes or until crispy and tender, flipping them over halfway through baking.
6. Serve the baked sweet potato fries as a healthy and tasty side dish.

Date _____

Daily Mood Tracker

This is a chart where you get to track how you're feeling each day. You can tag a smiley face if you're feeling happy, a sad face if you're feeling sad, or a neutral face if you're feeling indifferent. It's a fun way to see how your mood changes over time!

Excited ☐   Happy ☐   Relaxed ☐   Sad ☐   Nervous ☐   Stressed ☐   Angry ☐

Creative Visualization Exercise

Have you ever felt really happy and comfortable somewhere special, like your favorite park or your grandparent's house? Well, did you know that you can use your imagination to go there whenever you want?

Flying High:
Close your eyes and imagine that you're flying high in the sky. Maybe you're on a magic carpet or riding on the back of a dragon. Feel the wind rushing through your hair and the sun warming your skin. Enjoy the freedom of soaring through the air.

When you do creative visualization exercises, you can have fun imagining things while feeling calm and happy. Take a deep breath, close your eyes, and let your imagination take you on a wonderful adventure!

Colouring Time

Help colour in Ted
(you can also colour-in the title)

Date _____

Daily MOOd Tracker

This is a chart where you get to track how you're feeling each day. You can tag a smiley face if you're feeling happy, a sad face if you're feeling sad, or a neutral face if you're feeling indifferent. It's a fun way to see how your mood changes over time!

Excited☐ Happy☐ Relaxed☐ Sad☐ Nervous☐ Stressed☐ Angry☐

Sound Map

We're going to try something fun and exciting called "sound mapping." This activity will help you become more aware of the different sounds around you and how they are related to each other. By focusing on the sounds you hear and where they come from, you'll be practicing mindfulness and improving your listening skills. Plus, it's a great way to use your creativity and imagination!

To start, we'll need a piece of paper and some coloring tools like pencils, crayons, or markers. First, find a comfortable spot where you can sit and listen to the sounds around you. Close your eyes for a moment and take a few deep breaths to relax. Now, with your eyes open, start to listen carefully to all the sounds you hear. It could be birds singing, people talking, cars passing by, or even the wind rustling through the trees. Try to identify as many different sounds as you can.

Once you've identified the sounds, it's time to create your sound map. On your piece of paper, draw symbols or pictures to represent each sound you heard. For example, you can draw a bird for the bird singing or a car for the car passing by. As you draw, think about where each sound came from and place it on the map accordingly. This way, you're showing the spatial relationships between the sounds. When you're done, take a moment to look at your sound map and notice how all the sounds come together to create the unique soundscape of your environment.

Nature Walk

Mindfulness is a special way of paying attention to things around us. When we are mindful, we take time to notice what's going on inside our bodies and what's happening in the world around us. Walking in nature is a really great way to practice mindfulness!

When we walk in nature, we get to see so many amazing things - like big trees, colorful flowers, and little animals! We can use all of our senses to experience nature: we can smell the fresh air, feel the soft grass under our feet, hear the birds singing, and even taste the fresh berries growing on the bushes!

So, remember: going for a walk in nature and practicing mindfulness is a great way to feel more peaceful and happy. It's a chance to take a break from our busy lives and enjoy the beauty of the world around us.

Write a few words of what you saw and felt during your nature walk.

_____

_____

_____

_____

_____

_____

_____

_____

_____

_____

_____

_____

Date _____

Daily MOOd Tracker

This is a chart where you get to track how you're feeling each day. You can tag a smiley face if you're feeling happy, a sad face if you're feeling sad, or a neutral face if you're feeling indifferent. It's a fun way to see how your mood changes over time!

Excited ☐ Happy ☐ Relaxed ☐ Sad ☐ Nervous ☐ Stressed ☐ Angry ☐

Silly Face Meditation

We're going to try a super fun mindfulness activity called "Silly Face Meditation." It's all about making funny faces, but at the same time, we're going to pay attention to how our faces feel and the emotions each expression brings up. So, are you ready to get started and have some giggles?

First, find a comfortable spot to sit or stand where you can see yourself in a mirror. Take a few deep breaths to help you relax and focus. Now, let's start making some silly faces! You can scrunch up your nose, wiggle your eyebrows, puff out your cheeks, or even stick out your tongue. As you make each face, pay attention to how the muscles in your face feel. Does it feel tight or loose? Are there any funny sensations or tingles? Take your time to explore and have fun with each expression.

As you continue making silly faces, think about the feelings and emotions that come up. Does the face make you feel happy, surprised, or maybe even a little bit shy? It's okay if you start laughing or if you can't hold a face for too long - that's part of the fun! When you're ready, take another deep breath and let your face relax back to its normal position. Remember, Silly Face Meditation is not only about having fun, but also about learning to pay attention to our body and emotions.

Dreaming

When we dream, we tap into a world of endless possibilities and infinite potential.

Thoughts before sleep

_____
_____
_____

Emotions before sleep

_____

Dream

_____
_____
_____
_____
_____
_____
_____
_____
_____
_____
_____
_____
_____
_____
_____

Emotions after waking up from the dream

_____

Date _____

Daily Mood Tracker

This is a chart where you get to track how you're feeling each day. You can tag a smiley face if you're feeling happy, a sad face if you're feeling sad, or a neutral face if you're feeling indifferent. It's a fun way to see how your mood changes over time!

 Excited ☐ Happy ☐ Relaxed ☐ Sad ☐ Nervous ☐ Stressed ☐ Angry ☐

Gratitude Jar

Don't forget about your special treasure box where you put in little notes about things that make you happy or that you're grateful for. It's important because it helps you remember all the good things in your life, even when things feel tough. When you're feeling down, you can read through your notes and remember all the wonderful things you have in your life.

Goal Setting

Setting goals can help you build self-confidence and feel more in control of your life.

Which goals have you set and achieved so far?

_____

_____

_____

_____

_____

_____

_____

_____

How did accomplishing these goals make you feel?

_____

_____

_____

_____

_____

What are some goals that you would like to set for yourself? It could be something you want to learn, a skill you want to improve, or a task you want to complete. Make a list of things you would like to achieve!

☐ _____   ☐ _____

☐ _____   ☐ _____

☐ _____   ☐ _____

☐ _____   ☐ _____

☐ _____   ☐ _____

☐ _____   ☐ _____

☐ _____   ☐ _____

Date _____

Daily Mood Tracker

This is a chart where you get to track how you're feeling each day. You can tag a smiley face if you're feeling happy, a sad face if you're feeling sad, or a neutral face if you're feeling indifferent. It's a fun way to see how your mood changes over time!

Excited ☐   Happy ☐   Relaxed ☐   Sad ☐   Nervous ☐   Stressed ☐   Angry ☐

Daily Affirmations

Read Out Loud

I am capable of living life to the fullest
I am free from stress, anxiety, and negative thoughts
I am deserving of a happy and fulfilling life

Every day, our brains are learning and growing. When we say good things about ourselves, it helps our brains grow in a positive way. This makes it easier for us to learn new things and become smarter.

You might want to say these affirmations every day, like when waking up in the morning or before you go to bed at night. Or if you don't feel like saying them all the time, you might say them only when you need to feel better, like when you're feeling scared or sad.

It's up to you to decide how often you want to say these affirmations. What's most important is that you believe in the nice things you're saying to yourself and that they help you feel good inside.

So, remember: saying nice things to yourself is a great way to feel confident, strong, and loved!

Dreamcatcher

Materials:

A hoop (can be made from a wire, or you can use an embroidery hoop)
Yarn or string
Feathers
Beads
Scissors

Instructions:

1. Take the hoop and wrap it tightly with the yarn or string, you can use a peg to help keep the first end in please, wrap it until it is completely covered.
2. Tie a knot at the end of the string and start weaving it around the hoop. Make sure to keep the string taut as you weave.
3. As you weave, you can add beads to the string by sliding them onto the yarn and then weaving them in.
4. Once you've woven around the entire hoop, tie off the string with a knot and cut off any excess.
5. Take a piece of string and tie it onto the hoop, then add a feather to the end of the string.
6. Repeat step 5 with as many feathers as you'd like, making sure to space them out evenly around the hoop.
7. Once you've added all the feathers, you can hang the dreamcatcher in your room to catch bad dreams and promote peaceful sleep.

Remember, you can make your dreamcatcher as unique and colorful as you want by using different colors of yarn and beads. Have fun!

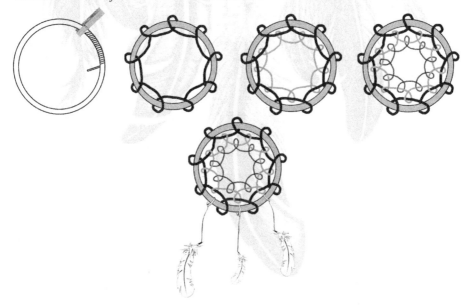

Date _____

Daily MOOd Tracker

This is a chart where you get to track how you're feeling each day. You can tag a smiley face if you're feeling happy, a sad face if you're feeling sad, or a neutral face if you're feeling indifferent. It's a fun way to see how your mood changes over time!

Excited ☐   Happy ☐   Relaxed ☐   Sad ☐   Nervous ☐   Stressed ☐   Angry ☐

Self-reflection

Take some time to think about how you're feeling and what's been going on in your life. Ask yourself "why did I tag myself with this emotion?", and write down your answer below.

_____
_____
_____
_____
_____
_____
_____
_____
_____
_____
_____
_____
_____
_____
_____
_____
_____
_____
_____
_____

Nature Mandala

Nature mandalas are a really cool activity that lets you use your imagination and connect with nature at the same time. First, go outside and look for pretty things like leaves, flowers, and stones. Once you have collected some, use them to create a beautiful pattern on the ground or a piece of paper. This pattern is called a mandala.

When you make a nature mandala, you get to use your creativity to arrange the materials in different ways. You can create any pattern you like! As you make your mandala, you can also take deep breaths and focus on the sounds and smells of nature around you. This will help you feel more calm and relaxed. When you're finished, you'll have a beautiful work of art that you can be proud of!

Check out the examples below. You can make them however you like, simply use your imagination!

Date _____

Daily MOOd Tracker

This is a chart where you get to track how you're feeling each day. You can tag a smiley face if you're feeling happy, a sad face if you're feeling sad, or a neutral face if you're feeling indifferent. It's a fun way to see how your mood changes over time!

Excited☐   Happy☐   Relaxed☐   Sad☐   Nervous☐   Stressed☐   Angry☐

Mindful Meditation

Guided meditation is a really cool way to practice mindfulness! When we meditate, we take a break from all the busy things around us and focus on our breathing and our thoughts. It's like taking a little break for our brains! Guided meditation is when someone talks to us while we meditate so don't forget to ask a parent, sibling or friend to help you.

Focusing on your breathing and counting 1...2....3...each inhale and exhale

Close your eyes and imagine a warm light surrounding your body, giving you a sense of comfort and peace

Imagine yourself in a peaceful place, like a beach or a forest, and listen to the sounds around you

Guides Notes

For children, it's often best to start with shorter meditation sessions and gradually increase the length as they become more comfortable with the practice. A good starting point for younger children might be just a few minutes per day, gradually increasing to 10-15 minutes as they become more comfortable with the practice.

It's important to remember that the quality of the meditation is more important than the quantity of time spent meditating. Even a short session of just a few minutes can be beneficial if it allows the child to focus their attention, calm their mind, and become more aware of their thoughts and feelings.

THE MAZE

Oh no! Peter has lost his way to his painting, help him find the way so he can create his masterpiece!

Date _____

Daily Mood Tracker

This is a chart where you get to track how you're feeling each day. You can tag a smiley face if you're feeling happy, a sad face if you're feeling sad, or a neutral face if you're feeling indifferent. It's a fun way to see how your mood changes over time!

Excited ☐ Happy ☐ Relaxed ☐ Sad ☐ Nervous ☐ Stressed ☐ Angry ☐

Coloring with Texture

Mindful Coloring with Texture is a fun way to explore your creativity and focus on your senses. To get started, you will need some textured materials like sandpaper, cotton balls, or bubble wrap, and some coloring materials like crayons, markers, or colored pencils.

Choose a textured material that you want to color on and place it on a flat surface. Then, choose your coloring materials and start coloring on the textured material. You can color in any pattern or design you like, but try to focus on the sensation of coloring on the different textures.

As you color, notice how the texture feels under your coloring tool. Is it bumpy? Smooth? Scratchy? Soft? Take deep breaths and focus on the sensation of coloring, letting yourself become fully absorbed in the experience.

When you're finished coloring, take a moment to appreciate your creation and the different textures you used. You can even display your artwork in a special place to remind you of the mindfulness exercise you just did!

Colouring Time

Help colour in Kitty
(you can also colour-in the title)

Date _____

Daily Mood Tracker

This is a chart where you get to track how you're feeling each day. You can tag a smiley face if you're feeling happy, a sad face if you're feeling sad, or a neutral face if you're feeling indifferent. It's a fun way to see how your mood changes over time!

Excited☐   Happy☐   Relaxed☐   Sad☐   Nervous☐   Stressed☐   Angry☐

Object Exploration

Mindful Object Exploration is a fun activity that you can do with a partner. To start, choose an object that you want to explore. It can be anything you like, such as a flower, a toy, or a rock.

Next, take a few deep breaths to help you focus. Hold the object in your hand and take a moment to really look at it. Notice its shape, color, and any other details that you can see.

Now, pass the object to your partner and ask them to describe how it feels in their hand. Is it hard, soft, smooth, or bumpy?

After your partner describes the feel of the object, take a turn smelling it. What does it smell like? Can you describe the scent?

Next, you can tap the object lightly and listen to the sound it makes. Does it make a loud sound or a soft sound?

Finally, take a moment to appreciate the object and express gratitude for it. Think about how it came to be and how it might be used or appreciated by others.

By exploring an object mindfully, you can learn to appreciate the little things in life and become more present in the moment. It's a great way to connect with your senses and your surroundings, and it's also a fun way to spend time with a friend or family member.

Nature Walk

Mindfulness is a special way of paying attention to things around us. When we are mindful, we take time to notice what's going on inside our bodies and what's happening in the world around us. Walking in nature is a really great way to practice mindfulness!

When we walk in nature, we get to see so many amazing things - like big trees, colorful flowers, and little animals! We can use all of our senses to experience nature: we can smell the fresh air, feel the soft grass under our feet, hear the birds singing, and even taste the fresh berries growing on the bushes!

Practicing mindfulness while we walk in nature helps us to be more present in the moment. We can take time to really look at and appreciate all the beauty around us. It can also help us feel calm and relaxed. Sometimes, when we are feeling upset or worried, walking in nature can help us feel better!

So, remember: going for a walk in nature and practicing mindfulness is a great way to feel more peaceful and happy. It's a chance to take a break from our busy lives and enjoy the beauty of the world around us.

Write a few words of what you saw and felt during your nature walk.

_____

_____

_____

_____

_____

_____

_____

Daily Mood Tracker

This is a chart where you get to track how you're feeling each day. You can tag a smiley face if you're feeling happy, a sad face if you're feeling sad, or a neutral face if you're feeling indifferent. It's a fun way to see how your mood changes over time!

Excited ☐   Happy ☐   Relaxed ☐   Sad ☐   Nervous ☐   Stressed ☐   Angry ☐

Mindful Body Scan

Mindful Body Scan is when you lie down on your back and focus on each part of your body. You can start at your toes and work your way up to your head, noticing any feelings or sensations in each part of your body. For example, you might notice your toes tingling, your legs feeling heavy, or your stomach feeling tight.

As you notice each sensation, you can take a deep breath in and imagine the air going to that part of your body. Then, as you exhale, you can imagine any stress or tension in that area melting away. This can help you feel more relaxed and calm.

It's like when you get a check-up at the doctor's office and they ask you to wiggle your toes and move your arms to make sure everything is working well. But instead of the doctor doing it, you get to do it yourself and it helps you feel better!

Lets Cook

Peanut Butter and Banana Smoothie

Shopping List

Bananas ☐
Unsweetened almond milk ☐
Peanut Butter ☐
Cinnamon ☐
Vanilla extract ☐
Ice cubes ☐

How to

Ingredients:
- 1 ripe banana
- 1/2 cup unsweetened almond milk
- 2 tablespoons natural peanut butter
- 1/2 teaspoon vanilla extract
- 1/2 teaspoon cinnamon
- 1 handful of ice cubes

1. Blend the banana, almond milk, peanut butter, vanilla extract, cinnamon, and ice cubes in a blender until smooth.
2. Pour the smoothie into a glass.
3. Serve immediately and enjoy!

Date _____

Daily Mood Tracker

This is a chart where you get to track how you're feeling each day. You can tag a smiley face if you're feeling happy, a sad face if you're feeling sad, or a neutral face if you're feeling indifferent. It's a fun way to see how your mood changes over time!

Excited☐   Happy☐   Relaxed☐   Sad☐   Nervous☐   Stressed☐   Angry☐

Creative Visualization Exercise

Have you ever felt really happy and comfortable somewhere special, like your favorite park or your grandparent's house? Well, did you know that you can use your imagination to go there whenever you want?

Future Self:
Close your eyes and imagine yourself as a grown-up. Think about what you want to be when you grow up and what kind of person you want to be. Imagine all the things you'll be able to do and how you'll feel when you achieve your goals.

Using your imagination in creative visualization exercises is a fun way to feel calm and happy. Take a deep breath, close your eyes, and let your mind take you on a exciting journey!

Goal Setting

When you set goals, you can measure your progress and celebrate your successes along the way.

Which goals have you set and achieved so far?

_____
_____
_____
_____
_____
_____
_____
_____

How did accomplishing these goals make you feel?

_____
_____
_____
_____
_____

What are some goals that you would like to set for yourself? It could be something you want to learn, a skill you want to improve, or a task you want to complete. Make a list of things you would like to achieve!

☐ _____   ☐ _____
☐ _____   ☐ _____
☐ _____   ☐ _____
☐ _____   ☐ _____
☐ _____   ☐ _____
☐ _____   ☐ _____
☐ _____   ☐ _____

Date _____

Daily MOOd Tracker

This is a chart where you get to track how you're feeling each day. You can tag a smiley face if you're feeling happy, a sad face if you're feeling sad, or a neutral face if you're feeling indifferent. It's a fun way to see how your mood changes over time!

Excited ☐   Happy ☐   Relaxed ☐   Sad ☐   Nervous ☐   Stressed ☐   Angry ☐

Daily Affirmations
Read Out Loud

I am at peace with myself and the world
I am grateful for my journey and trust it will lead me to success
I have a positive impact on the world and those around me

Sometimes we might feel sad or upset. But when we use daily affirmations, they can help us feel better. Saying things like, "I am loved and important," reminds us that we are special and cared for by our family and friends.

You might want to say these affirmations every day, like when waking up in the morning or before you go to bed at night. Or if you don't feel like saying them all the time, you might say them only when you need to feel better, like when you're feeling scared or sad.

It's up to you to decide how often you want to say these affirmations. What's most important is that you believe in the nice things you're saying to yourself and that they help you feel good inside.

So, remember: saying nice things to yourself is a great way to feel confident, strong, and loved!

Dreaming

Dreams are the keys to unlocking our full potential and realizing our true destiny.

Thoughts before sleep

_____
_____
_____

Emotions before sleep

_____

Dream

_____
_____
_____
_____
_____
_____
_____
_____
_____
_____
_____
_____
_____
_____

Emotions after waking up from the dream

_____

Date _____

Daily Mood Tracker

This is a chart where you get to track how you're feeling each day. You can tag a smiley face if you're feeling happy, a sad face if you're feeling sad, or a neutral face if you're feeling indifferent. It's a fun way to see how your mood changes over time!

Excited ☐   Happy ☐   Relaxed ☐   Sad ☐   Nervous ☐   Stressed ☐   Angry ☐

Head in the Clouds

Have you ever looked up at the sky and noticed how the clouds can form different shapes? That's what we're going to do today with an activity called "Cloud Storytelling." This fun and imaginative game will help you to see those clouds in a new way and use your creativity to make up exciting stories based on the shapes you see. It's a great way to practice using your imagination while being mindful of the beautiful world around you.

To get started, let's find a comfortable spot outside where you can see the sky clearly. Lie down on the grass or sit on a blanket, and take a few deep breaths, feeling the air filling your lungs as you breathe in and out. Now, look up at the clouds and try to find shapes that remind you of animals, objects, or anything else you can think of. Let your imagination run wild as you find different shapes! Remember, there are no right or wrong answers, just have fun and let your creativity soar.

Once you've found a cloud shape that interests you, it's time to create a story. Use your imagination to think about what that cloud character might be doing or where they might be going. Are they on an adventure? Maybe they're trying to solve a problem or find a new friend. As you weave your story, you can include other cloud shapes you see or even create a whole world for your character to explore. Share your story with a friend, family member, or even write it down in a journal. The more you practice, the better you'll become at creating exciting and imaginative stories.

Cloud storytelling is a wonderful way to build your storytelling skills while also learning to be present in the moment. As you focus on the shapes of the clouds and the world around you, you'll notice more details and find inspiration in the most unexpected places. Plus, by sharing your stories, you'll bring joy and entertainment to others as well.

So, next time you're outside and see some interesting clouds, remember to try cloud storytelling. Let your imagination take flight, and see where your cloud characters lead you. You might just find that you've discovered a whole new world of stories waiting to be told, all inspired by the beauty of nature's ever-changing canvas. Happy storytelling!

Mason Jar Lantern

Materials:

Mason jar
Tissue paper (colored or patterned)
White glue
Paintbrush
Scissors
Tea light candle or fairy lights (if possible an electrical one)

Instructions:

1. Cut the tissue paper into small squares or shapes.
2. Use the paintbrush to apply a thin layer of glue to the outside of the mason jar.
3. Stick the tissue paper pieces onto the jar, covering the entire surface. Overlapping is okay.
4. Apply another layer of glue over the tissue paper, making sure it is completely covered and sealed.
5. Let the jar dry completely (at least 2 hours).
6. Place a tea light candle or fairy lights inside the jar and light it up.

Enjoy your beautiful mason jar lantern as a night light or decoration!

Date _____

Daily Mood Tracker

This is a chart where you get to track how you're feeling each day. You can tag a smiley face if you're feeling happy, a sad face if you're feeling sad, or a neutral face if you're feeling indifferent. It's a fun way to see how your mood changes over time!

Excited ☐   Happy ☐   Relaxed ☐   Sad ☐   Nervous ☐   Stressed ☐   Angry ☐

Mindful Meditation

Guided meditation is a really cool way to practice mindfulness! When we meditate, we take a break from all the busy things around us and focus on our breathing and our thoughts. It's like taking a little break for our brains! Guided meditation is when someone talks to us while we meditate so don't forget to ask a parent, sibling or friend to help you.

Focusing on your breathing and counting 1...2...3...each inhale and exhale

Close your eyes and imagine a warm light surrounding your body, giving you a sense of comfort and peace

Imagine yourself in a peaceful place, like a beach or a forest, and listen to the sounds around you

Guides Notes

For children, it's often best to start with shorter meditation sessions and gradually increase the length as they become more comfortable with the practice. A good starting point for younger children might be just a few minutes per day, gradually increasing to 10-15 minutes as they become more comfortable with the practice.

It's important to remember that the quality of the meditation is more important than the quantity of time spent meditating. Even a short session of just a few minutes can be beneficial if it allows the child to focus their attention, calm their mind, and become more aware of their thoughts and feelings.

Mindful Storytelling

Have you ever heard of Mindful Storytelling? It's a fun activity where you get to create your own story that teaches you about being mindful. This means you can talk about being grateful, being kind to others, or anything else that helps you stay calm and happy.

Once you have your story ready, you can read it to your family and friends or write it down in a special journal. This way, you can remember how to be mindful even when you're not playing the game. So, let's get started on creating a story that's not only fun, but helps you be more mindful too!

_____

_____

_____

_____

_____

_____

_____

_____

_____

_____

_____

_____

_____

_____

_____

_____

_____

_____

_____

_____

_____

_____

_____

_____

_____

_____

_____

_____

Date _____

Daily MOOd Tracker

This is a chart where you get to track how you're feeling each day. You can tag a smiley face if you're feeling happy, a sad face if you're feeling sad, or a neutral face if you're feeling indifferent. It's a fun way to see how your mood changes over time!

Excited ☐   Happy ☐   Relaxed ☐   Sad ☐   Nervous ☐   Stressed ☐   Angry ☐

GratitUde Jar

Don't forget to add to your Gratitude Jar!
Your gratitude jar is important and it helps you appreciate the little things in life. It's easy to take things for granted, but when you start to write down the things that make you happy, you realize that even the small things can bring joy to your life. Maybe it's a warm hug from a loved one, a beautiful sunset, or your favorite meal. These little things are worth celebrating and remembering.

Colouring Time

Help colour in you new strange
friend that appeared in your vase
(you can also colour-in the title)

Date _____

Daily MOOd Tracker

This is a chart where you get to track how you're feeling each day. You can tag a smiley face if you're feeling happy, a sad face if you're feeling sad, or a neutral face if you're feeling indifferent. It's a fun way to see how your mood changes over time!

Excited ☐　　Happy ☐　　Relaxed ☐　　Sad ☐　　Nervous ☐　Stressed ☐　Angry ☐

Self-reflection

Take some time to think about how you're feeling and what's been going on in your life. Ask yourself "why did I tag myself with this emotion?", and write down your answer below.

_____
_____
_____
_____
_____
_____
_____
_____
_____
_____
_____
_____
_____
_____
_____
_____
_____
_____
_____
_____
_____
_____
_____

THE MAZE

Our unicorn friend can't find his way to his rainbow house. Give it a helping hand.

Date _____

Daily Mood Tracker

This is a chart where you get to track how you're feeling each day. You can tag a smiley face if you're feeling happy, a sad face if you're feeling sad, or a neutral face if you're feeling indifferent. It's a fun way to see how your mood changes over time!

Excited☐   Happy☐   Relaxed☐   Sad☐   Nervous☐   Stressed☐   Angry☐

Mindful Listening

"Mindful Listening." This game is all about using your ears to really pay attention to the sounds around you. Sometimes, we're so busy that we don't notice all the interesting noises in our environment. But with mindful listening, we'll learn to focus on these sounds and discover a whole new world that's right there waiting for us to explore!

To start playing, find a comfy spot to sit or lie down, somewhere you can be relaxed and comfortable. Once you're settled, close your eyes and take a few deep breaths. This will help you calm your mind and prepare for the game. Now, with your eyes closed, listen carefully to the sounds around you. You might hear the rustling of leaves, the hum of a refrigerator, or the distant sound of a car passing by. Remember, there are no right or wrong answers - the goal is to notice as many sounds as you can!

As you listen to the sounds, try to focus on the details of each one. What does it sound like? Is it high or low, loud or soft? Can you tell where the sound is coming from? Pay attention to how the sounds change over time, too - maybe they become louder, softer, or disappear altogether. Keep your ears open and your mind focused on the sounds for a few minutes. When you're ready, slowly open your eyes and return to the world around you. Congratulations, you've just practiced mindful listening! Remember, you can play this game anytime you want to tune in to the amazing world of sounds that surround us every day.

Nature Walk

Mindfulness is a special way of paying attention to things around us. When we are mindful, we take time to notice what's going on inside our bodies and what's happening in the world around us. Walking in nature is a really great way to practice mindfulness!

When we walk in nature, we get to see so many amazing things - like big trees, colorful flowers, and little animals! We can use all of our senses to experience nature: we can smell the fresh air, feel the soft grass under our feet, hear the birds singing, and even taste the fresh berries growing on the bushes!

Write a few words of what you saw and felt during your nature walk.

_____
_____
_____
_____
_____
_____
_____
_____
_____
_____
_____
_____
_____
_____

Date _____

Daily Mood Tracker

This is a chart where you get to track how you're feeling each day. You can tag a smiley face if you're feeling happy, a sad face if you're feeling sad, or a neutral face if you're feeling indifferent. It's a fun way to see how your mood changes over time!

Excited ☐ Happy ☐ Relaxed ☐ Sad ☐ Nervous ☐ Stressed ☐ Angry ☐

Daily Affirmations

Read Out Loud

I am constantly improving and growing every day
I have unlimited potential and unlimited possibilities
I am surrounded by love and support

Affirmations also help us be more patient and kind to ourselves. When we make mistakes, it's okay! Instead of feeling bad about it, we can say, "I am always learning and growing." This helps us forgive ourselves and keep trying our best.

You might want to say these affirmations every day, like when waking up in the morning or before you go to bed at night. Or if you don't feel like saying them all the time, you might say them only when you need to feel better, like when you're feeling scared or sad.

It's up to you to decide how often you want to say these affirmations. What's most important is that you believe in the nice things you're saying to yourself and that they help you feel good inside.

So, remember: saying nice things to yourself is a great way to feel confident, strong, and loved!

Lets Cook

Tuna Salad Wraps

Shopping List

Can of tuna ☐
Celery ☐
Red onion ☐
Greek yogurt (or light mayo) ☐
Whole wheat wraps ☐
Tomato ☐
Lettuce ☐

How to

Ingredients:
• 1 can of tuna, drained
• 1 stalk of celery, chopped
• 1/4 red onion, chopped
• 3 tablespoons plain Greek yogurt or light mayonnaise
• 3 whole wheat wraps
• 1 medium tomato, sliced
• 3 lettuce leaves

1. Drain the canned tuna and put it into a mixing bowl.
2. Add the chopped celery and red onion to the bowl.
3. Mix in 1 tablespoon of the Greek yogurt or light mayonnaise per person until the mixture is well combined.
4. Spread the tuna salad mixture onto the inside of each whole wheat wrap.
5. Top each wrap with tomato slices and a lettuce leaf.
6. Roll up the wrap and serve with carrot sticks or a side of fruit.

Date _____

Daily Mood Tracker

This is a chart where you get to track how you're feeling each day. You can tag a smiley face if you're feeling happy, a sad face if you're feeling sad, or a neutral face if you're feeling indifferent. It's a fun way to see how your mood changes over time!

Excited ☐ Happy ☐ Relaxed ☐ Sad ☐ Nervous ☐ Stressed ☐ Angry ☐

Creative Visualization Exercise

Have you ever felt really happy and comfortable somewhere special, like your favorite park or your grandparent's house? Well, did you know that you can use your imagination to go there whenever you want?

Superhero Adventure:
Imagine that you're a superhero with special powers. Maybe you can fly, run really fast, or become invisible. Picture all the adventures you'll have and all the people you'll help. Feel the power and confidence that comes with being a superhero.

Creative visualization exercises allow you to use your imagination and feel happy and relaxed. Take a deep breath, close your eyes, and let your thoughts take you on a fun-filled adventure!

Goal Setting

When you set goals, it's important to take action and work towards them every day, even if it's just a small step.

Which goals have you set and achieved so far?

_____
_____
_____
_____
_____
_____
_____
_____

How did accomplishing these goals make you feel?

_____
_____
_____
_____
_____

What are some goals that you would like to set for yourself? It could be something you want to learn, a skill you want to improve, or a task you want to complete. Make a list of things you would like to achieve!

☐ _____   ☐ _____
☐ _____   ☐ _____
☐ _____   ☐ _____
☐ _____   ☐ _____
☐ _____   ☐ _____
☐ _____   ☐ _____
☐ _____   ☐ _____

Date _____

Daily Mood Tracker

This is a chart where you get to track how you're feeling each day. You can tag a smiley face if you're feeling happy, a sad face if you're feeling sad, or a neutral face if you're feeling indifferent. It's a fun way to see how your mood changes over time!

Excited ☐   Happy ☐   Relaxed ☐   Sad ☐   Nervous ☐   Stressed ☐   Angry ☐

Loving-Kindness Meditation

This meditation helps us feel happier and more connected to others by focusing on sending positive thoughts and wishes to ourselves and the people around us. It's a wonderful way to practice being kind and loving to everyone, even to those we may not like very much.

To start, find a comfortable place to sit or lie down. Close your eyes and take a few deep breaths, feeling the air go in and out of your body. Now, imagine yourself surrounded by a warm, glowing light, like a big, cozy hug. Think about all the good things you wish for yourself - happiness, health, and love. Say to yourself, "May I be happy, may I be healthy, may I be safe, and may I be loved." Repeat these words a few times, letting the positive energy fill you up.

Next, think about your friends, family, or even people you don't know very well. Picture them surrounded by the same warm, glowing light, and send them your good wishes too. Say, "May you be happy, may you be healthy, may you be safe, and may you be loved." Finally, think about someone you may not like or someone you've had a disagreement with. This could be a little challenging, but remember that everyone deserves kindness. Picture them surrounded by the warm light and say, "May you be happy, may you be healthy, may you be safe, and may you be loved." By practicing loving-kindness meditation, you are spreading love and positivity to yourself and others, making the world a happier place.

Dreaming

Our dreams give us wings to soar to new heights and achieve the impossible.

Thoughts before sleep

_____
_____
_____

Emotions before sleep

_____

Dream

_____
_____
_____
_____
_____
_____
_____
_____
_____
_____
_____
_____
_____
_____

Emotions after waking up from the dream

_____

Date _____

Daily MOOd Tracker

This is a chart where you get to track how you're feeling each day. You can tag a smiley face if you're feeling happy, a sad face if you're feeling sad, or a neutral face if you're feeling indifferent. It's a fun way to see how your mood changes over time!

Excited ☐   Happy ☐   Relaxed ☐   Sad ☐   Nervous ☐   Stressed ☐   Angry ☐

Mindful Meditation

Guided meditation is a really cool way to practice mindfulness! When we meditate, we take a break from all the busy things around us and focus on our breathing and our thoughts. It's like taking a little break for our brains! Guided meditation is when someone talks to us while we meditate so don't forget to ask a parent, sibling or friend to help you.

Focusing on your breathing and counting 1...2...3...each inhale and exhale

Close your eyes and imagine a warm light surrounding your body, giving you a sense of comfort and peace

Imagine yourself in a peaceful place, like a beach or a forest, and listen to the sounds around you

Guides Notes

For children, it's often best to start with shorter meditation sessions and gradually increase the length as they become more comfortable with the practice. A good starting point for younger children might be just a few minutes per day, gradually increasing to 10-15 minutes as they become more comfortable with the practice.

It's important to remember that the quality of the meditation is more important than the quantity of time spent meditating. Even a short session of just a few minutes can be beneficial if it allows the child to focus their attention, calm their mind, and become more aware of their thoughts and feelings.

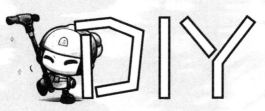

Tie-Dyeing a T-Shirt

Materials:

Plain white t-shirt
Rubber bands
Fabric dye (choose any colors you like)
Plastic gloves
Plastic bags
Large bowl or bucket
Water

Instructions:

1. Start by soaking the t-shirt in water, so it's damp but not dripping.
2. Lay the t-shirt flat on a clean surface, such as a table or the floor.
3. Pinch the center of the t-shirt and twist it into a spiral shape.
4. Use rubber bands to hold the spiral shape together. Wrap the bands tightly around the t-shirt, making sure they're evenly spaced.
5. Put on the plastic gloves to protect your hands from the dye.
6. Mix the fabric dye according to the instructions on the package in a large bowl or bucket.
7. Dip the twisted t-shirt into the dye, making sure to cover it completely.
8. Squeeze out the excess dye and put the t-shirt in a plastic bag.
9. Let the t-shirt sit in the bag for at least six hours, or as long as the dye instructions recommend.
10. Take the t-shirt out of the bag and rinse it thoroughly in cold water until the water runs clear.
11. Remove the rubber bands and wash the t-shirt in cold water with a mild detergent.
12. Let the t-shirt air-dry completely before wearing it.

Remember to have fun with it and experiment with different dye colors and patterns!

Date _____

Daily Mood Tracker

This is a chart where you get to track how you're feeling each day. You can tag a smiley face if you're feeling happy, a sad face if you're feeling sad, or a neutral face if you're feeling indifferent. It's a fun way to see how your mood changes over time!

Excited☐   Happy☐   Relaxed☐   Sad☐   Nervous☐   Stressed☐   Angry☐

Mirror Exercise

This exercise will help you understand your emotions better and become more aware of the different feelings you might experience throughout the day. It's a simple and enjoyable way to explore your emotions, and all you need is a mirror!

To start, find a mirror where you can see your face clearly. Stand or sit comfortably in front of it, take a deep breath, and relax. Now, think of different emotions, like happiness, sadness, anger, or surprise. For each emotion, try to make a facial expression that shows how you feel when you experience that emotion. For example, when you're happy, you might smile or laugh. Take your time and really focus on the feelings associated with each expression. It's okay if it takes a little practice to get the hang of it!

As you practice making different facial expressions, pay attention to how your face and body feel. Notice the changes in your muscles, the sensations around your eyes, mouth, and forehead, and any other feelings that come up. By doing this exercise, you'll become more in tune with your emotions and better at recognizing them in yourself and others. Remember, emotions are a natural part of life, and understanding them is a great skill to have.

Colouring Time

Help colour Louise's birthday party
(you can also colour-in the title)

Date _____

Daily Mood Tracker

This is a chart where you get to track how you're feeling each day. You can tag a smiley face if you're feeling happy, a sad face if you're feeling sad, or a neutral face if you're feeling indifferent. It's a fun way to see how your mood changes over time!

 Excited ☐ Happy ☐ Relaxed ☐ Sad ☐ Nervous ☐ Stressed ☐ Angry ☐

Heartbeat Awareness

Your heart is an amazing muscle that pumps blood all around your body. It beats many times a day to keep you healthy and strong. Heartbeat awareness is a way to focus on the rhythm and sensations of your heart, helping you to become more in tune with your body and feel calmer.

First, let's find your heartbeat. You can feel it by placing your hand on your chest or on your wrist. To find it on your wrist, use two fingers (your index and middle fingers) and press gently on the inside of your wrist, below the base of your thumb. You should feel a little tapping sensation; that's your heart beating! Now, close your eyes and take a few deep breaths. Try to relax and focus on the sensation of your heartbeat. Feel the rhythm as it goes "thump-thump" against your fingers.

Now that you've found your heartbeat, let's try counting it. Keep your fingers on your wrist or your hand on your chest. When you're ready, count the beats for 15 seconds. After 15 seconds, stop counting and multiply the number of beats you counted by 4. This will give you the number of beats per minute, which is your heart rate. You can do this activity whenever you need a moment of calm or just want to check in with your body. The more you practice, the more aware you'll become of your heartbeat and the sensations it creates. Enjoy connecting with your amazing heart!

THE MAZE

Mr Chompers forgot his way to the acorn, help him out!

Date _____

Daily Mood Tracker

This is a chart where you get to track how you're feeling each day. You can tag a smiley face if you're feeling happy, a sad face if you're feeling sad, or a neutral face if you're feeling indifferent. It's a fun way to see how your mood changes over time!

Excited ☐ Happy ☐ Relaxed ☐ Sad ☐ Nervous ☐ Stressed ☐ Angry ☐

Daily Affirmations
Read Out Loud

I am confident in my unique talents and gifts
I am worthy of love and respect from myself and others
I am always moving towards my highest good

Positive thoughts can make our days brighter and happier. When we wake up in the morning and start our day with affirmations like, "Today is going to be a great day," it helps us have a more positive attitude all day long.

You might want to say these affirmations every day, like when waking up in the morning or before you go to bed at night. Or if you don't feel like saying them all the time, you might say them only when you need to feel better, like when you're feeling scared or sad.

It's up to you to decide how often you want to say these affirmations. What's most important is that you believe in the nice things you're saying to yourself and that they help you feel good inside.

So, remember: saying nice things to yourself is a great way to feel confident, strong, and loved!

Dreaming

Dream big, work hard, stay focused, and surround yourself with good people who believe in you.

Thoughts before sleep

_____
_____
_____

Emotions before sleep

_____

Dream

_____
_____
_____
_____
_____
_____
_____
_____
_____
_____
_____
_____
_____
_____
_____

Emotions after waking up from the dream

_____

Date _____

Daily Mood Tracker

This is a chart where you get to track how you're feeling each day. You can tag a smiley face if you're feeling happy, a sad face if you're feeling sad, or a neutral face if you're feeling indifferent. It's a fun way to see how your mood changes over time!

Excited☐　　Happy☐　　Relaxed☐　　Sad☐　　Nervous☐　　Stressed☐　　Angry☐

Gratitude Jar

Don't forget to add to your Gratitude Jar!
A gratitude jar is also important because it helps you cultivate a positive mindset. When you start focusing on the good things in your life, you start to see more good things around you. It's like a positive snowball effect. You become more aware of the wonderful people, opportunities, and experiences in your life, and you start to feel more optimistic and hopeful about the future.

Nature Walk

Mindfulness is a special way of paying attention to things around us. When we are mindful, we take time to notice what's going on inside our bodies and what's happening in the world around us. Walking in nature is a really great way to practice mindfulness!

When we walk in nature, we get to see so many amazing things - like big trees, colorful flowers, and little animals! We can use all of our senses to experience nature: we can smell the fresh air, feel the soft grass under our feet, hear the birds singing, and even taste the fresh berries growing on the bushes!

Write a few words of what you saw and felt during your nature walk.

_____

_____

_____

_____

_____

_____

_____

_____

_____

_____

_____

_____

_____

_____

Date _____

Daily Mood Tracker

This is a chart where you get to track how you're feeling each day. You can tag a smiley face if you're feeling happy, a sad face if you're feeling sad, or a neutral face if you're feeling indifferent. It's a fun way to see how your mood changes over time!

Excited ☐ Happy ☐ Relaxed ☐ Sad ☐ Nervous ☐ Stressed ☐ Angry ☐

Self-reflection

Take some time to think about how you're feeling and what's been going on in your life. Ask yourself "why did I tag myself with this emotion?", and write down your answer below.

_____
_____
_____
_____
_____
_____
_____
_____
_____
_____
_____
_____
_____
_____
_____
_____
_____
_____
_____
_____
_____
_____
_____
_____

Lets Cook

Grilled Chicken Skewers

Shopping List

Chicken breasts ☐
Small onion ☐
Mushrooms ☐
Olive oil ☐
*Optional salt and pepper ☐

How to

Ingredients:
• 2 boneless, skinless chicken breasts, cut into bite-sized chunks
• 1 bell pepper, sliced into chunks
• 1 small onion, sliced into chunks
• 1 cup mushrooms, sliced
• 2 tablespoons olive oil
• Salt and pepper (optional)

1. Thread the chicken, bell peppers, onions, and mushrooms onto skewers.
2. Brush the skewers with the olive oil and sprinkle with salt and pepper (if desired).
3. Grill the skewers on medium-high heat for 10-15 minutes, or until the chicken is cooked through.
4. (optional) Serve with a side salad or whole grain bread.

Date _____

Daily MOOd Tracker

This is a chart where you get to track how you're feeling each day. You can tag a smiley face if you're feeling happy, a sad face if you're feeling sad, or a neutral face if you're feeling indifferent. It's a fun way to see how your mood changes over time!

Excited ☐   Happy ☐   Relaxed ☐   Sad ☐   Nervous ☐   Stressed ☐   Angry ☐

Creative Visualization Exercise

Have you ever felt really happy and comfortable somewhere special, like your favorite park or your grandparent's house? Well, did you know that you can use your imagination to go there whenever you want?

Colorful World:
Imagine a world where everything is colorful and bright. Picture all the colors of the rainbow and how they make you feel. Maybe you're walking on a rainbow or swimming in a sea of colors. Enjoy the beauty and joy of a colorful world.

When you do creative visualization exercises, you can use your imagination to feel happy and relaxed. Take a deep breath, close your eyes, and let your thoughts take you on a journey to a place where you feel safe, loved, and content.

Goal Setting

Remember that it's okay to change your goals as you grow and learn more about yourself and the world around you.

Which goals have you set and achieved so far?

_____
_____
_____
_____
_____
_____
_____
_____

How did accomplishing these goals make you feel?

_____
_____
_____
_____
_____

What are some goals that you would like to set for yourself? It could be something you want to learn, a skill you want to improve, or a task you want to complete. Make a list of things you would like to achieve!

☐ _____   ☐ _____
☐ _____   ☐ _____
☐ _____   ☐ _____
☐ _____   ☐ _____
☐ _____   ☐ _____
☐ _____   ☐ _____
☐ _____   ☐ _____

Date _____

Daily Mood Tracker

This is a chart where you get to track how you're feeling each day. You can tag a smiley face if you're feeling happy, a sad face if you're feeling sad, or a neutral face if you're feeling indifferent. It's a fun way to see how your mood changes over time!

Excited ☐   Happy ☐   Relaxed ☐   Sad ☐   Nervous ☐   Stressed ☐   Angry ☐

Mindful Meditation

Guided meditation is a really cool way to practice mindfulness! When we meditate, we take a break from all the busy things around us and focus on our breathing and our thoughts. It's like taking a little break for our brains! Guided meditation is when someone talks to us while we meditate so don't forget to ask a parent, sibling or friend to help you.

Focusing on your breathing and counting 1...2...3...each inhale and exhale

Close your eyes and imagine a warm light surrounding your body, giving you a sense of comfort and peace

Imagine yourself in a peaceful place, like a beach or a forest, and listen to the sounds around you

Guides Notes

For children, it's often best to start with shorter meditation sessions and gradually increase the length as they become more comfortable with the practice. A good starting point for younger children might be just a few minutes per day, gradually increasing to 10-15 minutes as they become more comfortable with the practice.

It's important to remember that the quality of the meditation is more important than the quantity of time spent meditating. Even a short session of just a few minutes can be beneficial if it allows the child to focus their attention, calm their mind, and become more aware of their thoughts and feelings.

Date _____

Daily MOOd Tracker

This is a chart where you get to track how you're feeling each day. You can tag a smiley face if you're feeling happy, a sad face if you're feeling sad, or a neutral face if you're feeling indifferent. It's a fun way to see how your mood changes over time!

Excited ☐   Happy ☐   Relaxed ☐   Sad ☐   Nervous ☐   Stressed ☐   Angry ☐

Nature Rubbings

Nature rubbings are a fantastic way to explore the outdoors and discover the beautiful textures and patterns all around us. This activity is not only enjoyable but also helps us practice mindfulness by paying close attention to the details and sensations we experience as we create our artwork.

To begin, let's gather our materials. You'll need some paper, like a sheet from your sketchbook or even regular printer paper, and a few crayons. Next, it's time to head outside and find some interesting textures to capture. You can look for tree bark, leaves, flowers, or even stones and rocks. Place your paper over the object you want to capture and hold it steady with one hand.

Now, grab a crayon and start gently rubbing it on the paper, directly over the texture you've chosen. Make sure you're using the side of the crayon, not the tip. As you rub, you'll notice the pattern of the object appearing on your paper like magic! Focus on the sensations and patterns that emerge as you create your nature rubbing. Feel the crayon gliding over the paper and the different textures underneath. Keep exploring and creating rubbings of various objects you find in nature. Remember to take your time, enjoy the process, and pay attention to the details in your artwork.

Have fun, and don't forget to share your nature rubbings with your friends and family!

THE MAZE

Our friend needs to get back in her ship before she runs out of oxygen. Help her find the way

Date _____

Daily MOOd Tracker

This is a chart where you get to track how you're feeling each day. You can tag a smiley face if you're feeling happy, a sad face if you're feeling sad, or a neutral face if you're feeling indifferent. It's a fun way to see how your mood changes over time!

Excited ☐   Happy ☐   Relaxed ☐   Sad ☐   Nervous ☐   Stressed ☐   Angry ☐

Daily Affirmations

Read Out Loud

I am filled with positivity and optimism
I trust in my abilities and decisions
I am grateful for all the blessings in my life

Daily affirmations teach us to be proud of who we are. We all have special talents and skills. By saying things like, "I am proud of my unique gifts," we learn to appreciate ourselves and celebrate our differences.

You might want to say these affirmations every day, like when waking up in the morning or before you go to bed at night. Or if you don't feel like saying them all the time, you might say them only when you need to feel better, like when you're feeling scared or sad.

It's up to you to decide how often you want to say these affirmations. What's most important is that you believe in the nice things you're saying to yourself and that they help you feel good inside.

So, remember: saying nice things to yourself is a great way to feel confident, strong, and loved!

Dreaming

Dreams are the foundation of our reality. Without them, we are aimless and lost.

Thoughts before sleep

_____
_____
_____
_____

Emotions before sleep

_____

Dream

_____
_____
_____
_____
_____
_____
_____
_____
_____
_____
_____
_____
_____
_____
_____

Emotions after waking up from the dream

_____

Daily Mood Tracker

This is a chart where you get to track how you're feeling each day. You can tag a smiley face if you're feeling happy, a sad face if you're feeling sad, or a neutral face if you're feeling indifferent. It's a fun way to see how your mood changes over time!

Excited ☐   Happy ☐   Relaxed ☐   Sad ☐   Nervous ☐   Stressed ☐   Angry ☐

Candle Gazing

This exercise will help you focus your mind and relax your body. It's a great way to practice mindfulness by paying close attention to the candle's flame, its colors, movement, and the warmth it gives off. Don't worry, we'll make sure to do this safely, so let's get started!

First, we need to set up the space for our candle gazing. Find a comfortable and quiet spot where you can sit on the floor or a cushion. Make sure you're away from anything that could catch fire. Now, ask an adult to help you light a candle and place it at a safe distance in front of you. Once the candle is lit, sit down and take a few deep breaths to relax your body and mind.

Now, it's time to start gazing at the candle's flame. Look at the different colors you see in the flame. Do you see blue, yellow, or maybe even a little bit of orange? Notice how the flame moves and dances in the air. Can you feel the warmth coming from the candle? As you watch the flame, try to let go of any thoughts that come into your mind. Just focus on the colors, movement, and warmth of the candle. If your mind starts to wander, that's okay! Just gently bring your attention back to the flame. You can practice this for a few minutes, and when you're ready to finish, ask an adult to help you blow out the candle. Great job practicing mindfulness with candle gazing!

Simple Friendship Bracelet

Materials:

Embroidery floss or colorful string
Scissors

Instructions:

1. Cut 3 strands of embroidery floss or string to about 30cm long
2. Tie the 3 strands together in a knot at one end, leaving a small loop at the top.
3. Secure the knotted end to a table or clipboard with tape or a safety pin.
4. Separate the strands so that one color is on the left, one in the middle, and one on the right.
5. Take the string on the left and place it over the middle string.
6. Then, take the string on the right and place it over the left string, and under the middle string.
7. Pull the strings tight, making sure they are all aligned in the middle.
8. Repeat steps 5-7, alternating between the left and right strings until the bracelet is long enough to fit around your wrist.
9. Tie a knot at the end, leaving a small loop.
10. Cut off any excess string.

These bracelets make great gifts for friends or family members and are a fun way to practice mindfulness and creativity.

You can also add beads or other items to the bracelet, your imagination has no limits!

B A C   B C A   C B A

Date _____

Daily Mood Tracker

This is a chart where you get to track how you're feeling each day. You can tag a smiley face if you're feeling happy, a sad face if you're feeling sad, or a neutral face if you're feeling indifferent. It's a fun way to see how your mood changes over time!

Excited☐ Happy☐ Relaxed☐ Sad☐ Nervous☐ Stressed☐ Angry☐

Feather Balancing

Feather balancing is all about finding balance and focus, while we pay close attention to our breath and the way the feather moves. This exercise will help you feel more relaxed, and you'll also learn how to concentrate better. Are you ready to give it a try?

First, find a soft and light feather. Hold the feather gently between your thumb and index finger, and then carefully place it on the tip of your other index finger. Now, take a deep breath in through your nose and slowly breathe out through your mouth. Keep your eyes on the feather and try to balance it on your fingertip. It might wobble a little, and that's okay! The goal is to keep the feather from falling off your finger for as long as you can. Remember to keep breathing slowly and calmly as you do this.

If the feather starts to wobble too much or falls off, don't worry! Just pick it up and try again. Each time you practice, you'll get better at balancing the feather and focusing on your breath. This is a great exercise to do whenever you feel stressed or need a break from your day. As you become more skilled at feather balancing, you'll notice that your concentration and mindfulness improve too. So, have fun with this activity and remember to stay patient and focused!

Goal Setting

Remember that setbacks are a natural part of achieving your goals. Don't be discouraged if you encounter obstacles along the way!

Which goals have you set and achieved so far?

_____
_____
_____
_____
_____
_____
_____
_____

How did accomplishing these goals make you feel?

_____
_____
_____
_____
_____

What are some goals that you would like to set for yourself? It could be something you want to learn, a skill you want to improve, or a task you want to complete. Make a list of things you would like to achieve!

☐ _____   ☐ _____
☐ _____   ☐ _____
☐ _____   ☐ _____
☐ _____   ☐ _____
☐ _____   ☐ _____
☐ _____   ☐ _____
☐ _____   ☐ _____

Date _____

Daily Mood Tracker

This is a chart where you get to track how you're feeling each day. You can tag a smiley face if you're feeling happy, a sad face if you're feeling sad, or a neutral face if you're feeling indifferent. It's a fun way to see how your mood changes over time!

Excited☐   Happy☐   Relaxed☐   Sad☐   Nervous☐   Stressed☐   Angry☐

Creative Visualization Exercise

Have you ever felt really happy and comfortable somewhere special, like your favorite park or your grandparent's house? Well, did you know that you can use your imagination to go there whenever you want?

Beach Vacation:
Close your eyes and imagine that you're on a relaxing beach vacation. Picture the sand between your toes, the sound of the waves, and the warm sun on your skin. Feel yourself relaxing and letting go of any stress or worries.

Creative visualization exercises are a great way to use your imagination and feel calm and joyful. Take a deep breath, close your eyes, and let your mind take you on an adventure full of wonder and excitement!

Nature Walk

Mindfulness is a special way of paying attention to things around us. When we are mindful, we take time to notice what's going on inside our bodies and what's happening in the world around us. Walking in nature is a really great way to practice mindfulness!

When we walk in nature, we get to see so many amazing things - like big trees, colorful flowers, and little animals! We can use all of our senses to experience nature: we can smell the fresh air, feel the soft grass under our feet, hear the birds singing, and even taste the fresh berries growing on the bushes!

Write a few words of what you saw and felt during your nature walk.

_____

_____

_____

_____

_____

_____

_____

_____

_____

_____

_____

_____

_____

_____

_____

_____

Date _____

Daily Mood Tracker

This is a chart where you get to track how you're feeling each day. You can tag a smiley face if you're feeling happy, a sad face if you're feeling sad, or a neutral face if you're feeling indifferent. It's a fun way to see how your mood changes over time!

Excited ☐   Happy ☐   Relaxed ☐   Sad ☐   Nervous ☐   Stressed ☐   Angry ☐

Daily Affirmations

Read Out Loud

I am worthy and deserving of happiness
I am strong and capable of overcoming any challenge
I am loved and appreciated just as I am

Daily affirmations help us build healthy habits for our whole life. When we start saying nice things about ourselves when we are young, it becomes a habit we carry with us as we grow up. This helps us become happier and more successful adults.

You might want to say these affirmations every day, like when waking up in the morning or before you go to bed at night. Or if you don't feel like saying them all the time, you might say them only when you need to feel better, like when you're feeling scared or sad.

It's up to you to decide how often you want to say these affirmations. What's most important is that you believe in the nice things you're saying to yourself and that they help you feel good inside.

So, remember: saying nice things to yourself is a great way to feel confident, strong, and loved!

Lets Cook

Veggie Pita Pockets

Shopping List

Whole wheat pita pockets ☐
Carrots ☐
Cucumbers ☐
Bell peppers ☐
Hummus or avocado spread ☐
*Optional pieces of chicken or turkey for non-veggie option ☐

How to

Ingredients:
- 3 whole wheat pita pockets
- 1 large carrot, sliced
- 1 small cucumber, sliced
- 1 bell pepper, sliced
- 1/4 cup hummus or avocado spread
- 3 slices of turkey or chicken (optional)

1. Cut up the vegetables into small, bite-sized pieces
2. Spread 1 tablespoon of the hummus or avocado spread onto the inside of each pita pocket
3. Stuff the vegetables and turkey or chicken slices (if using) into the pita pocket. Serve and enjoy!

Date _____

Daily Mood Tracker

This is a chart where you get to track how you're feeling each day. You can tag a smiley face if you're feeling happy, a sad face if you're feeling sad, or a neutral face if you're feeling indifferent. It's a fun way to see how your mood changes over time!

Excited ☐　　Happy ☐　　Relaxed ☐　　Sad ☐　　Nervous ☐　　Stressed ☐　　Angry ☐

Mindful Meditation

Guided meditation is a really cool way to practice mindfulness! When we meditate, we take a break from all the busy things around us and focus on our breathing and our thoughts. It's like taking a little break for our brains! Guided meditation is when someone talks to us while we meditate so don't forget to ask a parent, sibling or friend to help you.

Focusing on your breathing and counting 1...2...3...each inhale and exhale

Close your eyes and imagine a warm light surrounding your body, giving you a sense of comfort and peace

Imagine yourself in a peaceful place, like a beach or a forest, and listen to the sounds around you

Guides Notes

For children, it's often best to start with shorter meditation sessions and gradually increase the length as they become more comfortable with the practice. A good starting point for younger children might be just a few minutes per day, gradually increasing to 10-15 minutes as they become more comfortable with the practice.

It's important to remember that the quality of the meditation is more important than the quantity of time spent meditating. Even a short session of just a few minutes can be beneficial if it allows the child to focus their attention, calm their mind, and become more aware of their thoughts and feelings.

Dreaming

Don't let anyone tell you that you can't achieve your dreams. Believe in yourself and go after what you want.

Thoughts before sleep

_____
_____
_____

Emotions before sleep

_____

Dream

_____
_____
_____
_____
_____
_____
_____
_____
_____
_____
_____
_____
_____
_____

Emotions after waking up from the dream

_____

Date _____

Daily MOOd Tracker

This is a chart where you get to track how you're feeling each day. You can tag a smiley face if you're feeling happy, a sad face if you're feeling sad, or a neutral face if you're feeling indifferent. It's a fun way to see how your mood changes over time!

Excited ☐   Happy ☐   Relaxed ☐   Sad ☐   Nervous ☐   Stressed ☐   Angry ☐

Self-reflection

Take some time to think about how you're feeling and what's been going on in your life. Ask yourself "why did I tag myself with this emotion?", and write down your answer below.

_____
_____
_____
_____
_____
_____
_____
_____
_____
_____
_____
_____
_____
_____
_____
_____
_____
_____
_____
_____
_____
_____

Colouring Time

Kitty has been busy popping bubbles, want to help it be more colourful?
(you can also colour-in the title)

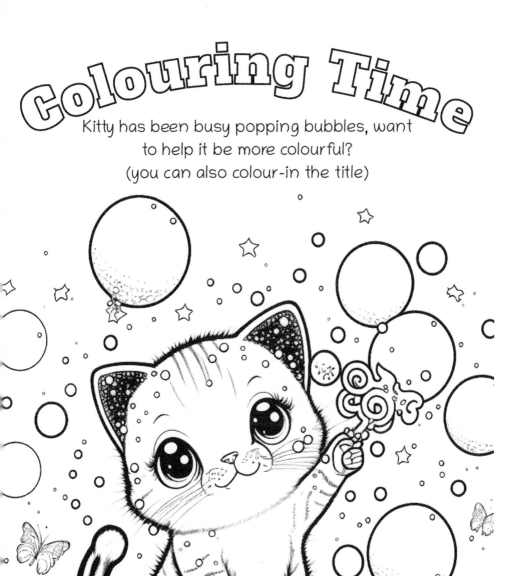

We've reached the end of our mindfulness adventure and we hope you had a fantastic time discovering all the amazing activities in this book. Along the way, we learned how to focus our minds, explore our emotions, and appreciate the world around us in a whole new way.

As you journey through life, remember that mindfulness is a powerful tool to help you stay present, calm, and connected to yourself and others. Keep practicing the activities you enjoyed the most and don't be afraid to try new ones, too. The world is full of wonderful surprises waiting for you to uncover.

Thank you for joining us on this incredible adventure, and remember: you are strong, kind, and capable of amazing things. Now go out there, spread your wings, and let your inner light shine bright!

With love and warm wishes

The Peartrees

P.S. - We left a little space for you to write whatever you would like to add to this amazing activity book you now completed. For example, you can write back to us and tell us how you felt reaching the end of this journey, or create a small short story of your journey.

"Blank spaces are the canvas of infinite possibilities, where creativity and imagination are free to paint their own masterpieces." - Unknown

Printed in Great Britain
by Amazon

21183804R00088